Sermons for the Saints

Dudley Weaver

Parson's Porch Books
www.parsonsporchbooks.com

Sermons for the Saints
ISBN: Softcover 978-1-949888-16-4
Copyright © 2018 by Dudley Weaver

All rights reserved. No part of this book may be reproduced or transmitted in any form or by any means, electronic or mechanical, including photocopying, recording, or by any information storage and retrieval system, without permission in writing from the publisher.

Sermons for the Saints

Contents

Foreword 9

Preface 11

Who Is in Charge Here? 13
   Job 38:1-7, 34-41

Mary's Radical Song 20
   Luke 1:39-55

Repentance 26
   Luke 3:1-6

A Moment of Unmistakable Clarity 32
   Luke 9:28-36

So, You Want to Follow 38
   Mark 8:27-38

A Wandering Aramean Was My Father 44
   Deuteronomy 26:1-5; Luke 4:1-13

The Kingdom of God Is Like 51
   Mark 4:26-34

"Hope" 56
   Jeremiah 33:14-16

Finding Your Life's Calling 62
   Jeremiah 1:4-10

Snap Judgements 68
   John 1:43-51

Impossible, Simply Impossible 73
   John 6:1-14

Bread of Life 79
    John 6:24-35
Jumping Ship 85
    John 6:56-59
A Listening Presence 90
    Mark 5:21-34
Seeing with Clarity 96
    Mark 10:46-52
And Taking First Place Is 101
    Mark 9:30-37
Competition or Cooperation? 107
    Mark 9:38-41
Forgiveness Is Never Cheap 113
    Luke 7:36-8:3
Facing Formidable Foes 120
    Mark 4:35-41
Where Are You God? 126
    Exodus 17:1-7
Seeing Clearly 132
    John 9:1-33
The Road to Emmaus 139
    Luke 24:13-35
A Cruel Story 145
    Genesis 21:8-21

Who Belongs Here?..151
   Genesis 37:1-4, 12-28; Romans 10:5-15
Johnny Come Lately 158
   Matthew 20:1-16
Practicing Love 164
   John 15:9-17
Dry Bones 169
   John 11:1-45
Crossing Over Jordan 176
   Joshua 3:7-17
In Communion with the Saints 182
   1 Thessalonians 4:13-18

Foreword

In the past fifty years, preaching in mainline denominations has become a reflection of America's culture wars. On the one side are ministers who proclaim the Bible's unquestioned authority in the face of modernism; on the other, those who promote social justice at the cost of detaching Christianity from its biblical roots. And herein lies a danger, for in taking sides in such misguided animosity Christians make biblical Christianity increasingly irrelevant for the modern world. It is, therefore, cause for celebration when a minister's faith leads him or her to envision a middle ground between these extremes. And in this collection of sermons, Dr. Dudley Weaver does just that.

While he preaches from the Bible, Weaver does not preach the Bible, but the gospel in the Bible. Likewise, when he condemns social injustice, which he does in no uncertain terms, his weapon of choice is the good news of salvation, not political solutions or a misplaced confidence in the goodness of people. As a result, Weaver is able to address the real causes of social injustice: human choice, greed, prejudice, selfishness, self-deception, neglect, and fear—in a word, sin. Moreover, he directs his message at precisely those people whom God has empowered to do something about it: Christians.

The sermons in this collection take on big issues like appreciating moments of clarity for what they bring, determining the cost of forgiveness, and deciding who's in charge. As Weaver knows, however, there is no easy fix for sin. While change—true, meaningful change—is a gift from God, it begins within an individual's heart and demands sacrifice, hope, hard decisions, and faith. There is no attempt here to take the edge off of Jesus' demands, no inclination toward a comfortable understanding of scripture. Indeed, Weaver often suggests that scripture is a mirror that reflects and even amplifies a believer's shortcomings before God. Yet he is also quick to illustrate sin using his own conceits and failures, giving readers the confidence that their guide is himself guided by a yearning to understand, a humility before God's grace, and an anticipation of the resurrection.

A talented writer and insightful theologian himself, Weaver also shows himself to be an attentive student of such authors as Frederick Buechner, Kathleen Norris, Wallace Alston, Dietrich Bonhoeffer, and Eugene Peterson, among others.

Will Deming, PhD. is Professor of Theology at the University of Portland, Portland, Oregon, and author of *Rethinking Religion: A Concise Introduction*, among other publications. He is an active member, teacher, and elder in First Presbyterian Church, Portland.

Preface

I am grateful for this opportunity to share some of the work that I have prayed and labored over for more than forty years. Try as I might, I have never completed a sermon manuscript and thought to myself: "There, it's done." Sermons, I believe, are, by the power of the Holy Spirit, more than completed manuscripts or extemporaneous words—eloquent or simple—proclaimed by the preacher, but a means by which God speaks a word that sometimes challenges, frequently comforts, and always communicates the good news of what God has done and is doing through Jesus Christ in our lives and the life of the world.

I would be remiss if I did not thank David Russell Tullock for the invitation to submit these sermons for publication, my friend Will Deming for his kind words in the Foreword to this book, and my wife Mary Schutt Weaver, who edited the manuscript and who for almost fifty years has encouraged me, listened to me Sunday after Sunday, and gently offered constructive criticism along the way. Being a preacher's spouse is no easy task, and she has fulfilled her role with grace, humor, and steadfastness. I owe a tremendous debt of gratitude to the late Elizabeth Achtemeier, who taught me and others homiletics at Union Theological Seminary in Virginia. Her voice has echoed in my mind many times as I crafted Sunday sermons.

Preaching is always a two-way street: one proclaims while others listen. I am grateful to the members and friends of

Hodges Presbyterian Church, Hodges, SC; Westminster Presbyterian Church, Columbia, SC; First Presbyterian Church, Savannah, Georgia; Westminster Presbyterian Church, Charleston, SC; First Presbyterian Church, Portland Oregon; and Memorial Presbyterian Church, St. Augustine, Florida, for their attentiveness, encouragement, honesty, and, when needed, forgiveness. I have been deeply blessed.

Who Is in Charge Here?
Job 38:1-7, 34-41

Then the Lord answered Job out of the whirlwind:
'Who is this that darkens counsel by words without knowledge?
Gird up your loins like a man,
  I will question you, and you shall declare to me.

'Where were you when I laid the foundation of the earth?
  Tell me, if you have understanding.
Who determined its measurements—surely you know!
  Or who stretched the line upon it?
On what were its bases sunk,
  or who laid its cornerstone
when the morning stars sang together
  and all the heavenly beings shouted for joy?

'Can you lift up your voice to the clouds,
  so that a flood of waters may cover you?
Can you send forth lightnings, so that they may go
  and say to you, "Here we are"?
Who has put wisdom in the inward parts,
  or given understanding to the mind?
Who has the wisdom to number the clouds?
  Or who can tilt the waterskins of the heavens,
when the dust runs into a mass
  and the clods cling together?

'Can you hunt the prey for the lion,
  or satisfy the appetite of the young lions,
when they crouch in their dens,
  or lie in wait in their covert?
Who provides for the raven its prey,
  when its young ones cry to God,
  and wander about for lack of food?

You know, sometimes when it rains it pours. In Job's case, the proverbial rain came down in an overwhelming torrent that washed away his family, his home, his wealth, his health—everything of value to him. Things became so bad that at one point, having watched, day after day, his suffering and his brooding over how this all could have happened to him his wife suggested, "Why don't you curse God, and die?" "Just get it over with, for God's sake."

Job was a good man, an exemplary man. He was faithful to God and fair with his neighbors. A finer man you could never meet, but Job was also a man of his time, and according to the thinking of his time, the only explanation for his suffering was that he had offended God in some way. Job could not imagine what he had done or had failed to do that could possibly warrant this measure of suffering. If he could only have a few minutes of the Almighty's time he could straighten all this out, explain how God had made a terrible mistake! Indeed, much of the Book of Job centers on this quest for an audience with God. God's silence, though, is deafening, and his absence perplexing. Job complains, "If I go forward, he is not there, or backward, I cannot perceive him; on the left he hides, and I cannot behold him; I turn to the right, but I cannot see him." (23:8,9) If only God would give him an audience, he could explain, he could set the record straight, and things in his life would return to the way they were supposed to be—the life of a righteous man.

When Job gets his audience with God, it is not at all what he expected. Before he can raise his voice in complaint, ask even the first question, the Lord has some questions of his own. "Who is this that darkens counsel by words without knowledge? Gird up your loins like a man, I will question you, and you shall declare to me. Where were you when I laid the foundations of the earth? Tell me, if you have understanding. Who determined its measurements—surely you know . . . Have you commanded the morning since your days began, and caused the dawn to know its place . . . have you entered into the springs of the sea, or walked in the recesses of the deep . . . Can you bind the chains of the Pleiades, or loose the cords of Orion . . . Can you lift up your voice to the clouds, so that a flood of waters may cover you . . . Can you hunt prey for the lion, or satisfy the appetite of young lions?" Job impertinently responds that he has said all that he is going to say. The Lord then resumes the questioning and at last gets to the point, "Will you put me in the wrong? Will you condemn me that you may be justified?" (40:8) which is to say, "Who do you think you are?"

There have been times when I, too, have raised my voice in anger to God, times when I have wondered, "If there is a God in heaven, how can this be happening? It is so unjust, so unfair! I mean some things people bring upon themselves, but this? God, you have it all wrong!" I know that God is not the author of our pain, but you look at the world in which we live and you wonder, you really wonder—has God checked out? Is he just not paying attention, or does he not care? Is God, after all, really God? Where is the evidence of his majesty, power, and might? From all appearances it is the opposition that holds the power, who is calling the shots. For us, like Job, sometimes it makes no sense, no sense at all. If God would only hear us, heed our wisdom, do as we know is right then all would be set in order again. If we were in charge, things would be different.

In some respects, of course, we are in charge, but not as the owners. We are, rather, only stewards or managers of the gifts of life and creation. Our responsibility is not to do whatever we may think is right or what is most advantageous to us, but to steward the gift according to the owner's intent and purpose. We, though, continue to delude ourselves into thinking that we really can create the biblical tower of Babel, which is to say that if we only throw enough money, technology, science, energy, power, or brute force at a problem or a need, we can fix anything and achieve anything. God breaks Job's stony and stubborn silence with a challenge: "Have you an arm like God, and can you thunder with a voice like his? Deck yourself with majesty and dignity; clothe yourself with glory and splendor. Pour out the overflowing of your anger and look on all who are proud and abase them. Look on all who are proud and bring them low; tread down the wicked where they stand. Hide them all in the dust together; bind their faces in the world below. Then I will also acknowledge to you that your own right hand can give you victory." (40:9-14) In other words, "Come on, give being God a try," and we *have*, with disastrous results. Ever since the woman first plucked the forbidden fruit in the garden and gave some to her husband and they both ate, we have been caught up in the struggle that issues from the attempt to be god to ourselves and god of the universe. We forget, both individually and corporately, that we are the creatures, not the Creator; the subjects not the Sovereign. We are part of the problem, not its sole solution.

Our presence here each Lord's Day is a confession on our part that we ourselves cannot gain the victory. Our presence here is an acknowledgement of our need for God in our lives and the life of the world. Here we confess our failures and reach for God's forgiveness. Here we are nurtured in God's word and feast upon the bread of life. Here we are renewed in the paschal mystery of Christ, for every Sunday is a commemoration of our Lord's suffering, death, and resurrection, and every Sunday is affirmation of his exaltation to glory and his rule in creation. Every Sunday we give witness to the conviction that, as the hymn puts it, "though the wrong seems oft so strong, God is the ruler yet." The world is not at all what God intends for it to be. We live in a broken, conflicted world where bad things happen to good people; where evil ones too often go unpunished; where hunger, homelessness, injustice, and acts of unspeakable cruelty apparently go unchecked, and where what peace there may be is always a fragile and never quite complete reality. That's the reality of the world, but there is a counter-reality that assures us that God is at work in Christ to redeem the world and the people of God's making. God is at work to put down the powers opposed to his will, to heal what is wounded, to bind up what is broken, indeed, to make all things new, even when we may not ourselves be able to see it.

How, then, do we live in this time between the times, this time between the inauguration of God's sovereign rule on earth and its ultimate fulfillment when the Lord of creation returns in his glory? Job's friends sought to comfort him with pious platitudes, telling him what he ought to do—which was easy for them to do because none of them was in his shoes. In fact, none of them ever really drew close to his pain. While pious platitudes are certainly not foreign to the followers of Jesus, it is not to platitudes that Jesus calls us, but to the proclamation of the good news of what God has done and is doing in the world through him and to its incarnation as we enter into the world's pain, bearing his love through the gift of our love and his presence through the gift of our presence, prayers, acts of kindness, and deeds of mercy. Jesus drew close to the pain, close enough to touch it and to be touched by it, and so he calls us to do.

You and I are not in charge, but we know who is, and it is with faith in him that we live our lives, love and serve our neighbors, and anticipate that time when God's will is done on earth as it is in heaven.

Mary's Radical Song
Luke 1:39-55

In those days Mary set out and went with haste to a Judean town in the hill country, where she entered the house of Zechariah and greeted Elizabeth. When Elizabeth heard Mary's greeting, the child leapt in her womb. And Elizabeth was filled with the Holy Spirit and exclaimed with a loud cry, 'Blessed are you among women, and blessed is the fruit of your womb. And why has this happened to me, that the mother of my Lord comes to me? For as soon as I heard the sound of your greeting, the child in my womb leapt for joy. And blessed is she who believed that there would be a fulfilment of what was spoken to her by the Lord.'

And Mary said,
'My soul magnifies the Lord,
   and my spirit rejoices in God my Saviour,
for he has looked with favour on the lowliness of his servant.
   Surely, from now on all generations will call me blessed;
for the Mighty One has done great things for me,
   and holy is his name.
His mercy is for those who fear him
   from generation to generation.
He has shown strength with his arm;
   he has scattered the proud in the thoughts of their hearts.
He has brought down the powerful from their thrones,
   and lifted up the lowly;

> *he has filled the hungry with good things,*
> *and sent the rich away empty.*
> *He has helped his servant Israel,*
> *in remembrance of his mercy,*
> *according to the promise he made to our ancestors,*
> *to Abraham and to his descendants forever.'*

Mary was little more than a child, at least by our standards. Her voice, I imagine, bore the sweetness of youth, an angel's whisper all bathed in sweet light, innocent, pure and pristine. Yet the song that comes from her lips on this occasion is anything but sweetness and light. It is a radical song that springs from the heart of one who is convinced that the child within her womb is the one chosen by God to turn things around in this world. Mary is so certain that the lyrics are cast in the past tense. "He has shown strength within his arm; he has scattered the proud in the thoughts of their heart. He has brought down the powerful from their thrones and lifted up the lowly; he has filled the hungry with good things and sent the rich away empty." The song portrays a radical reversal of roles—the proud are humiliated and the powerful deposed while the lowly are exalted. The poor receive an abundance of good things and the rich are turned away empty-handed. That is what the future holds under Mary's child, the "Son of the Most High."

Only someone who has been at the bottom of the heap can appreciate the sentiments of Mary's song. The man or woman working two jobs and doing his or her best to support a family; the person living in his car; the family forced to flee from their home and community by the onslaught of a godless, even demonic enemy; the man or woman denied justice, the victim of sexual abuse or other forms of personal violence can understand. Most of us, though, at least those of us in this room, have no way of understanding. We simply haven't been there.

In some respects, this song of Mary's judges us, for we are not the poor, but the wealthy; we are not the weak, but the powerful. This passage, along with the Sermon on the Plain in Luke's Gospel, assumes that the poor are the friends of God and the wealthy are God's enemies. "Blessed are you who are poor, for yours is the kingdom of God . . . but woe to you who are rich, for you have received your consolation. Blessed are you who are hungry now, for you will be filled . . . Woe to you who are full now, for you will be hungry." (Luke 6:20b, 24, 21a, 25a) While the scriptures consistently show an affinity on God's part for the poor and the powerless, it never is quite that simple, is it? Being poor doesn't necessarily make you right with God, any more than being wealthy necessarily sets you at odds with God.

While it may not be a simple reversal of roles, the inauguration of the kingdom of Mary's son does spell a radical reorientation of the values and priorities of the world. The things that matter most in his kingdom are not the things that matter most in this world. In the rule that he has come to establish, love is far more than an emotion, but the operating principle in all relationships and actions.

Justice is not merely something to be sought, but realized, and the shalom of God, the peace of God which is wholeness within and without, fills human life and community. Fear is banished. Want is a thing of the past. Truthfulness can rightly be assumed in human relationships. Jealousy, dishonesty, resentment, thievery, murder and war have no place. Sin—that power that separates us from God and from one another—is conquered.

It sounds like a pipe dream, but already the kingdom of God's love in Christ is taking shape and being realized, not through the power of arms, political coercion, threats or intimidation that are so much a part of the human arsenal, but through the transformation of human hearts and human community, one human being at a time. Philip Brooks' lovely carol reminds us: "How silently, how silently, the wondrous gift is given! So God imparts to human hearts the blessings of his heaven. No ear may hear his coming, but in this world of sin, where meek souls will receive him, still the dear Christ enters in." His rule is established not from the outside in, but from the inside out. You and I are its citizens, and in and through us and our sisters and brothers across the globe, the kingdom of our Lord and Savior Jesus Christ rises to meet, to challenge, and to transform the kingdoms of this world.

In a prayer often attributed to Archbishop Oscar Romero, but written by Bishop Ken Untener of Saginaw, Michigan, in 1979 as a reflection on the anniversary of the Salvadoran archbishop's martyrdom, we are reminded: "It helps, now and then, to step back and take a long view. The kingdom is not only beyond our efforts, it is even beyond our vision. We accomplish in our lifetime only a tiny fraction of the magnificent enterprise that is God's work. Nothing we do is complete, which is a way of saying that the Kingdom always lies beyond us. No statement says all that could be said. No prayer fully expresses our faith. No confession brings perfection. No pastoral visit brings wholeness. No program accomplishes the Church's mission. No set of goals and objectives includes everything. This is what we are about. We plant the seeds that one day will grow. We water seeds already planted, knowing that they hold future promise. We lay foundations that will need further development. We provide yeast that produces far beyond our capabilities. We cannot do everything, and there is a sense of liberation in realizing that. This enables us to do something, and to do it very well. It may be incomplete, but it is a beginning, a step along the way, an opportunity for the Lord's grace to enter and do the rest. We may never see the end results, but that is the difference between the master builder and the worker. We are workers, not master builders; ministers, not messiahs. We are prophets of a future not our own."[1]

Mary's song is our song, too, for it belongs to all whose lives have been touched by the grace and love of the child of her womb. Admittedly, it is sometimes easier for us to sing than

---

[1] United States Conference of Catholic Bishops, www.usccb.org

at other times, and, to be honest, there are times when we lose its tune and confuse its lyrics, but the tune and its words linger in our hearts and call us back again and again to the life and place of our true belonging—the Kingdom of God.

Repentance
Luke 3:1-6

In the fifteenth year of the reign of Emperor Tiberius, when Pontius Pilate was governor of Judea, and Herod was ruler of Galilee, and his brother Philip ruler of the region of Ituraea and Trachonitis, and Lysanias ruler of Abilene, during the high-priesthood of Annas and Caiaphas, the word of God came to John son of Zechariah in the wilderness. He went into all the region around the Jordan, proclaiming a baptism of repentance for the forgiveness of sins, as it is written in the book of the words of the prophet Isaiah,

> *'The voice of one crying out in the wilderness:*
> *"Prepare the way of the Lord,*
> *make his paths straight.*
> *Every valley shall be filled,*
> *and every mountain and hill shall be made low,*
> *and the crooked shall be made straight,*
> *and the rough ways made smooth;*
> *and all flesh shall see the salvation of God."*

He must have been quite a sight to behold, this prophet who kept to the wilderness. He wore a garment made of camel's hair secured with a leather belt around his waist and survived on a diet of locusts and wild honey. While curiosity may have drawn some into the wilderness to hear him preach, when he began to speak the novelty of his appearance and the eccentricity of his lifestyle were eclipsed by the power of his proclamation. John's message was clear, direct, and compelling. The time was coming and soon would be when the Lord's anointed one would appear. Now was the time to get ready. But how?

Years ago, when my wife was packing for a trip to London with her mother, our five-year-old daughter asked: "Do you think you will see the Queen?" "No," her mother answered, "but if we were to see her, what do you think we ought to do?" Thinking our daughter would answer "bow or curtsy," she was surprised when she said: "You better get your act together!" That is essentially what John had to say to those who came to hear him. He urged his listeners to get their acts together. He spoke not necessarily what they wanted to hear, but what they needed to hear. He touched the depths of their beings, not with words of soothing comfort and easy assurance, but with words that challenged their accustomed ways of being and doing and summoned them to a radical redirection in their lives. "Repent!" he adjured them. Turn around, make an about-face, go in a different direction in your life and conduct. In other Gospel accounts of John's preaching specific directions were given to specific groups. "What must we do?" asked the crowds. "Whoever has two coats must share with anyone who has none; and whoever has food must do likewise," he told them. To the tax collectors he said: "Collect no more than the amount prescribed for you." And to the soldiers who came to him, he exhorted: "Do not extort money from anyone by threats or false accusation and be satisfied with your wages." Now, none of these practices would have seemed out of the ordinary to John's listeners. It's just the way things were. If one coat is good, surely two are better. And what does it hurt to fudge an extra half per cent on what the government allows you to collect in your district? It isn't like you are making a killing on the government standard. And what could be so wrong with using your authority as a Roman soldier to make your life a little easier among these folks in the backwash of the civilized world? It wasn't as if you asked to be assigned here, and everyone did it.

You see, what John brought to the forefront with his listeners were not the worst mistakes they might ever have made or the deep secrets they kept under wraps, but the day-to-day deficiencies in their lives and conduct—the things they never thought twice about and perhaps could not readily see. When I read a text like this, I wonder about those things in my life as well—the things that have become so much a part of who I am that I'm not consciously aware of them: ingrained prejudices, unacknowledged wrongs, easy judgments. Frederick Buechner wrote: "It is important to tell at least from time to time the secret of who we truly and fully are—even if we tell it only to ourselves—because otherwise we run the risk of losing track of who we truly and fully are and little by little come to accept instead the highly edited version which we put forth in hope that the world will find it more acceptable than the real thing."[2] John

---

[2] Frederick Buechner, *Telling Secrets: A Memoir*, (Harper One, 2000), 2, 3

called upon his hearers to look at themselves, really look at themselves, and so his words call us today.

"Repent; turn around." It sounds simple enough, but it is neither simple nor easy. We hang onto possessions, habits, practices, perspectives, and prejudices which we know are just plain wrong because of the harm they do to others and the harm they do to us as well. But these things have a way of becoming a part of who we are and letting go of them is like entering into a forbidding wilderness of unknown challenges and dangers. When I finally gave up smoking more than two decades ago, my greatest anxiety was not the break with the chemical dependency, but with the emotional dependency. My pack of cigarettes was my constant companion and, in some ways, my best friend. Life without it had become unimaginable. When I was nervous, I would light up; when I was bored, I would light up; when I was relaxing, I would light up; when I needed to concentrate, I would light up. The first thing I did in the morning was to light up and the last thing I did before bed was to light up. It's amazing how easily you can justify something that you know is wrong for you and wrong for others. The choice to break with an addiction; to risk trust after your trust has been betrayed; to accept yourself for who you are rather than who others expect you to be; to let go of old wrongs done to you; to strive to see yourself fully and completely may well bring you into a wilderness filled with all sorts of unknown and unseen perils. Yet only as we travel through that wilderness can we emerge into the freedom of new life. It is only as we let go of the old life that we can embrace the new.

Those who went into the wilderness to hear John, who were convicted by his words and were baptized, emerged from the water not only with the assurance that God had forgiven them, but with a resolve to live new lives. They pledged to open their hearts to others and to share; tax collectors vowed to resist the graft that ran rampant in their profession by collecting only what was their due, and soldiers promised to refrain from abusing their authority by taking advantage of the local people. Their repentance, they pledged, would take tangible form. Good intentions, though, are not always enough, are they? You try hard. You put your heart and your soul into whatever it is that needs changing in your life, and sometimes, despite your best efforts, it just doesn't work. The difference between John and the one whose coming he proclaimed was that Jesus does more than show us the error of our ways and encourage us to try harder. Jesus walks to meet us and promises to walk with us through the wilderness into the new life for which we yearn.

When the going is challenging, when the choices are difficult, when your own resolve may weaken, remember these words of St. Paul to the Christians at Philippi: "I am confident of this, that the one who began a good work among you will bring it to completion by the day of Jesus

Christ." It is in this hope that we live and that we face the challenges of life. Thanks be to God.

A Moment of Unmistakable Clarity
Luke 9:28-36

Now about eight days after these sayings Jesus took with him Peter and John and James and went up on the mountain to pray. And while he was praying, the appearance of his face changed, and his clothes became dazzling white. Suddenly they saw two men, Moses and Elijah, talking to him. They appeared in glory and were speaking of his departure, which he was about to accomplish at Jerusalem. Now Peter and his companions were weighed down with sleep; but since they had stayed awake, they saw his glory and the two men who stood with him. Just as they were leaving him, Peter said to Jesus, 'Master, it is good for us to be here; let us make three dwellings, one for you, one for Moses, and one for Elijah'—not knowing what he said. While he was saying this, a cloud came and overshadowed them; and they were terrified as they entered the cloud. Then from the cloud came a voice that said, 'This is my Son, my Chosen; listen to him!' When the voice had spoken, Jesus was found alone. And they kept silent and in those days told no one any of the things they had seen.

In a slim little book entitled *Why Preach? Why Listen?* William Muehl writes: "It is incorrect, I am persuaded, to believe as many do today that the problem with idolatry is the tendency to identify the wrong things as God. That is, we make a god of money or power or sex or status and so on. The crux of the problem is not, I suggest, the identification of the wrong thing as God, but the very process of attempting to identify the divine in particular terms, the effort to cram the massively complex nature of the Most High into some single principle of interpretation."[3] Muehl is, I think, painfully correct.

In our Gospel lesson this morning Peter, James, and John, in one overwhelming moment, come face to face with the awesome majesty of the transcendent Christ. On the mountain where they had gone to pray, Jesus' appearance was transfigured before them and they saw not only Jesus the teacher, the healer, the man of compassion and grace, but the one of whom the apostle John wrote: "In the beginning was the Word, and the Word was with God, and the Word was God." Awe came over them, and Peter, who was known to speak first and only later to think about what he said, proposed that they build three dwellings there on the mountain, one for the Christ, and one for Moses and one for Elijah, who had appeared with him. Like the followers of Jesus in the centuries afterwards, Peter sought to reduce the awesome majesty and holiness of the eternal Christ to something that would fit within the parameters of his expectation and understanding, something that could even be housed.

While Peter's suggestion was embarrassingly naïve, we can't be too hard on him, for we, too, are inclined to confine God to the limits of our expectations, experience, and desires. God is a Presbyterian, Baptist, Congregationalist, Methodist, Roman Catholic, or whatever. God is a left-

---

[3] William Muehl, *Why Preach: Why Listen*, (Fortress Press, 1986)

leaning liberal or a right-wing reactionary; a Democrat or Republican; a sexual libertarian or sexual ascetic, a proponent of gay marriage or a stalwart opponent of the same. And, if we don't define the Holy Other in terms of our theology, ecclesiology, or political ideology, then it is in terms of our own experience. Those who *really* know God have felt God's presence in the warmth of their hearts and the power of emotional experience. Those who *really* know God keep a rein on their emotions, for they know that human emotions are fickle, and that God is best known and served through the utilization of the mind and the intellect.

God is not bound by the articles of religious dogmatism, that is true. But at the same time, the reality that is God cannot be confined to the rumination of the human heart, as in the "spiritual but not religious" phenomenon of the 21st century. Some years ago, Robert Bellah coined the term Sheilaism for this form of spirituality. In his book "Habits of the Heart" he wrote: "Sheila Larson is a young nurse who has received a good deal of therapy and describes her faith as 'Sheilaism.' This suggests the logical possibility of more than 235 million American religions, one for each of us. 'I believe in God,' Sheila says. 'I am not a religious fanatic. [Notice at once that in our culture any strong statement of belief seems to imply fanaticism, so you have to offset that.] I can't remember the last time I went to church. My faith has carried me a long way. It's Sheilaism. Just my own little voice.'"[4] Very often that "little voice from within" is supplemented by a selection of practices and beliefs from a cafeteria of spiritual offerings. You take a little of this and a little of that and fashion a self-designed spirituality that works for you. God is what you want god to be and changes as your needs may change. It's easy to judge, but these are people struggling with the deep spiritual hunger which is common to all humanity. As St. Augustine noted long ago: "Our souls are restless till they find their rest in thee." There is a fundamental yearning within the human spirit for a reconnection to the divine, but these folks are simply misguided in their search.

God wills that we should know him—not merely about him—but know him, and to that end God has made himself known to us in a multitude of ways. The majesty and beauty of the created order point us in the direction of God. "The heavens are telling the glory of God; and the firmament proclaims his handiwork," exults the psalmist. "Day to day pours forth speech, and night to night declares knowledge. There is no speech, nor are there words; their voice is not heard; yet their voice goes out through all the earth, and their words to the end of the world." (Psalm 19:1-4a) Yet, while creation may point us in the direction of God, creation is insufficient for us to know God. Again, and again in the course of human history God has entered into our time, our circumstances, and our need to make himself known. The

---

[4] Robert N. Bellah, ed., *Habits of the Heart: Individualism and Commitment in American Life* (Berkeley, CA: University of California Press, 1985), 221

Bible is the story of that divine/human interaction. In the calling of Abraham and God's covenant in him; in God's hearing the cries of the Hebrew slaves in Egypt and in sending Moses to liberate them; in God's covenant promises to them and through them to the world; in the cry of the prophets calling them back to God when they had wandered, and ultimately in the birth cry of a child in the village of Bethlehem, God has entered into our world and our lives to make himself known. The miracle of the incarnation is that the holy otherness of God has taken human form. The majesty, splendor, and power of God have come to reside among us in the fragile life of a newborn child. In his life, his teaching, his character and daily walk, his death and resurrection the "massively complex nature of the Most High" has taken human form. In him God has drawn near to us and shared the burdens, the joys, and the uncertainties of human life. In him God has shown us his face, touched us with his love, and claimed us to be his own. While creation, spiritual practices, and even other religious texts may point us in the direction of God, it is in Jesus Christ, God's own Son, that God has revealed himself to us most fully and authentically.

Peter would have stayed in the splendor of the mountaintop away from the pain and the harsh realities of human life. I can understand that. It was on the mountain that their faith in Jesus as the Christ, the Son of the living God, had been irrefutably confirmed and everything seemed crystal clear, but just as they savored that supreme moment of revelation,

Jesus surprised them by leading them back down the mountain to the plain below, to the reality of daily life where things are not always black and white but often shrouded in gray; where faith is tried and tested; where things don't always make sense; where life can be painfully unpredictable, but this is where discipleship is lived. Going back to the plain and continuing the journey to what would be a cross was not at all what they thought the Christ was all about, but it was as they followed him and listened to him, as the voice from above had adjured them, that their understanding was deepened, their faith was strengthened, and their lives were transformed in ways they never imagined possible. Christ came to be formed in them; Christ came to be seen in them.

In the end, you see, it is not we who define God, but God who defines us. It is not we who shape God, but God who shapes us in and through Jesus Christ, and that is done not in the glory of the mountaintop, but in the walk of daily life.

So, You Want to Follow
Mark 8:27-38

Jesus went on with his disciples to the villages of Caesarea Philippi; and on the way he asked his disciples, 'Who do people say that I am?' And they answered him, 'John the Baptist; and others, Elijah; and still others, one of the prophets.' He asked them, 'But who do you say that I am?' Peter answered him, 'You are the Messiah.' And he sternly ordered them not to tell anyone about him.

Then he began to teach them that the Son of Man must undergo great suffering, and be rejected by the elders, the chief priests, and the scribes, and be killed, and after three days rise again. He said all this quite openly. And Peter took him aside and began to rebuke him. But turning and looking at his disciples, he rebuked Peter and said, 'Get behind me, Satan! For you are setting your mind not on divine things but on human things.'

He called the crowd with his disciples, and said to them, 'If any want to become my followers, let them deny themselves and take up their cross and follow me. For those who want to save their life will lose it, and those who lose their life for my sake, and for the sake of the gospel, will save it. For what will it profit them to gain the whole world and forfeit their life? Indeed, what can they give in return for their life? Those who are ashamed of me and of my words in this adulterous and sinful generation, of them the Son of Man will also be ashamed when he comes in the glory of his Father with the holy angels.'

There are some things so foreign to our way of thinking and doing, so far beyond the realm of our expectation as to make them unimaginable, but that doesn't mean they can't happen. When the unimaginable crashes into our lives, things as they are supposed to be get turned upside-down and inside-out, and nothing makes sense anymore. Such was the case for the disciples in our reading this morning.

The twelve men who had answered Jesus' call to "follow me" had left home, family, work, and security behind in order to follow him. They had been waiting for him, for that one whose appearing would mark the inauguration of the Messianic kingdom where wrongs are righted, and God's rule prevails in all the earth. Their vision of what that means was quite different from his. They looked for a conquering hero who would unseat "the powers that be" and would establish a new regime, and they fully anticipated appropriate rewards for their faith, their efforts, indeed their sacrifices in following Jesus. They dreamed of and argued among themselves about places of authority and power that should be theirs in the coming kingdom. That's the way things are supposed to work in the world. So you can imagine their utter confusion in the scene drawn for us in today's reading from the Gospel of Mark.

It began with a simple question: "Who do people say that I am?" And they told Jesus what they had been hearing: Some say, "John the Baptist; and others, Elijah; and still others, one of the prophets." Honest and safe answers they were. But then he asked a far more personal question: "Who do you say that I am?" Not "What does the voice of public opinion or the latest statement by the religious authorities have to say," but "Who do you say that I am?" It was Peter who answered for them: "You are the Messiah." But rather than the "high-fives" all around that the disciples might have expected when they gave the right answer, the conversation took a serious turn. Jesus "began to teach them that the Son of Man must undergo great suffering, and be rejected by the elders, the chief priests, and the scribes, and be killed, and after three days rise again." That wasn't what they expected! That wasn't what they had signed on for! You see, while Peter and his colleagues got the answer right, what they understood about Messiah and what Jesus understood were eons apart. Indeed, it was so radically different from what they expected that Peter took Jesus aside and rebuked him. "This is no way for you to be talking, Lord! For God's sake, get your act together!" And Jesus turned his back to him and speaking to the eleven, he said: "Get behind me, Satan! For you are setting your mind not on divine things but on human things." What you have in mind, what you envision is not at all what God intends. Don't tempt me with your designs!

That was bad enough, but then Jesus went on to warn: "If any want to become my followers, let them deny themselves and take up their cross and follow me." Who in their right mind would want to follow him on those terms? I mean it's one thing to go about trying to do good; it's one thing to work at forgiving your enemy; it's one thing to deny yourself a little from time to time, but taking up a cross? I don't think so! Every human instinct recoils at the thought of that kind of sacrifice. And so, like Peter, not wanting to leave off following Jesus altogether, we urge him to be a bit more reasonable in his expectations. How are you going to build a following or maintain a following with those kinds of expectations? We want to take the edge off of Jesus' demands, present the good news of the Gospel in more palatable terms, smooth down its rough places so that it might be more acceptable. We want to redesign Jesus in our image rather than being ourselves changed into his. But Jesus is insistent; there is no other way: "If any want to become my followers, let them deny themselves, take up their cross, and follow me."

You see, we don't have the option of choosing to be a cross-bearing Christian or a non-cross-bearing Christian, like we might choose to be a Presbyterian or Lutheran Christian, a liberal or conservative Christian. Each of us in choosing to follow Jesus takes up the cross or we are not following Jesus. The cross meets us, wrote Dietrich Bonhoeffer, not as "the terrible end to an otherwise god-fearing and happy life," but it meets us at the beginning of the Christian life." "When Christ calls [us] He bids [us] come and die. It may be a death like that of the first disciples who had to leave home and work to follow Him, or it may be a death like Luther's, who had to leave the monastery and go out into the world. But it is the same death every time—death in Jesus Christ, the death of the old [person] at His call." [5]

To bear the cross is to say no to yourself so that you may say yes to Jesus. To bear the cross is to die with Christ so that you may also be raised with him not only in the end time, but in the present time. It is to die to every mean impulse, to every distortion to the image of God within you so that Christ's own life may come to be seen in your living and loving and relating. That will lead you to take up other crosses that, if were not for the cross of Christ, you might well leave lying behind: the child in your classroom—the difficult one or troubled one or ugly one; the older man down the street who's beginning to struggle with dementia and with whom it is hard to carry on a conversation but who needs someone to listen; or the cause in the community that isn't as popular as other causes but is just as important in its own way. We ordinarily think of a cross as something that is thrust upon us, something which we have no other choice but to bear, but our cross, as the cross our Savior bore, is a matter of choice. You can take it up or walk away.

The paradox of the Christian gospel is that it is only as we deny ourselves the place of central importance in life and in obedience to Jesus take up the cross and follow him—walk in his ways and live in his truth—that we really come to life and grow into that fullness of life and peace and joy which

---

[5] Dietrich Bonhoeffer, *The Cost of Discipleship*, (The Macmillan Company, NY, © 1948), 73

Jesus promises to those who embrace him and his love. We ordinarily think of our lives as vessels to be filled with more and more stuff, larger and grander experiences. The more you have, the better your life will be, the world assures us. What we discover, though, is that the more we have, the more we think we need. Consequently, we never have all we need. The desire for more is an insatiable one. Jesus offers something quite contrary to the world's point of view. The gain in life, the very way to life, is not through holding and hoarding, but through opening up and sharing; it is not through walking away from the pain and difficulties of the world around us, but through entering into them in his name.

"Those who want to save their life will lose it, and those who lose their life for my sake, and for the sake of the gospel will save it." Thanks be to God. Amen.

A Wandering Aramean Was My Father
Deuteronomy 26:1-5; Luke 4:1-13

Deuteronomy 26:1-5

When you have come into the land that the Lord your God is giving you as an inheritance to possess, and you possess it, and settle in it, you shall take some of the first of all the fruit of the ground, which you harvest from the land that the Lord your God is giving you, and you shall put it in a basket and go to the place that the Lord your God will choose as a dwelling for his name. You shall go to the priest who is in office at that time, and say to him, 'Today I declare to the Lord your God that I have come into the land that the Lord swore to our ancestors to give us.' When the priest takes the basket from your hand and sets it down before the altar of the Lord your God, you shall make this response before the Lord your God: 'A wandering Aramean was my ancestor; he went down into Egypt and lived there as an alien, few in number, and there he became a great nation, mighty and populous.

Luke 4:1-13

Jesus, full of the Holy Spirit, returned from the Jordan and was led by the Spirit in the wilderness, where for forty days he was tempted by the devil. He ate nothing at all during those days, and when they were over, he was famished. The devil said to him, 'If you are the Son of God, command this stone to become a loaf of bread.' Jesus answered him, 'It is written, "One does not live by bread alone."'

Then the devil led him up and showed him in an instant all the kingdoms of the world. And the devil said to him, 'To you I will give their glory and all this authority; for it has been given over to me, and I give it to anyone I please. If you, then, will worship me, it will all be yours.' Jesus answered him, 'It is written,
"Worship the Lord your God and serve only him."'
Then the devil took him to Jerusalem, and placed him on the pinnacle of the temple, saying to him, 'If you are the Son of God, throw yourself down from here, for it is written,
"He will command his angels concerning you to protect you", and 'On their hands they will bear you up,
  so that you will not dash your foot against a stone."'
Jesus answered him, 'It is said, "Do not put the Lord your God to the test."' When the devil had finished every test, he departed from him until an opportune time.

A wandering Aramean was my father; he went down into Egypt and lived there as an alien." For whatever reason that sentence has always had a certain appeal to me. I don't know precisely why, but maybe it is the sense of adventure that accompanies the idea of being a "wandering Aramean"—moving from one place to the next, seeking new experiences, discovering new places and people. It all sounds so adventuresome—a kind of "Westward, Ho!" or "Lost in Space" experience. However, the thought of wandering about with no place to call home, not really knowing where you are going next, and never quite being sure what tomorrow will bring, while exciting, is also a bit unnerving, at least to me. Of course, some folks spend their lives that way—moving from one job to the next, from one spouse to the next, from one home to another—hoping, always hoping that the next time or the next place will be the one where the treasure for which they have been searching will be found. Most of us, though, are a little more self-directed than that. We at least have an idea of where we are going and what we want to do with our lives. We may change directions from time to time along the way, but we know where we ultimately want to be.

I think that was as true of Jesus as it is of all of us. He lived at home until he was almost thirty years old, plying his trade, we assume, as a carpenter. Over those years it is reasonable to suppose that there was within him a dawning awareness both of who he was and of what he was to do. John the Baptizer's call to "repent, for the Kingdom of God is at hand," signaled for Jesus the time to act. Laying aside his carpenter's tools, he made his way to the Jordan, where he was baptized by the prophet. At his baptism his identity was clearly revealed: "You are my beloved Son; with you I am well pleased," but what that would mean for him was another matter entirely: entitlement, power, wealth, success? The time in the wilderness that followed his baptism was a time not merely of testing, but also a time of discernment in which these questions were answered, and his ministry began to take shape.

"If you are the Son of God, command this stone to become bread," the devil challenged him. Jesus would know want.

Would he use his power to fulfill his personal needs and desires? "And the devil took him up and showed him all the kingdoms of the world in a moment of time and said to him, 'If you will worship me, it will all be yours.'" Jesus would know the temptation to use his power for political gain. "If you are the Son of God, throw yourself down from here; for it is written: 'he will give his angels charge of you, to guard you.'" Jesus would know the temptation to exploit his relationship with the Father for public acclaim. Luke tells us that when "the devil had ended every temptation, he departed from him until an opportune time." This was not the end of the struggle between his will and his Father's. It would continue into the very shadow of his cross. That is the nature of Christian discipleship as well. We live in the tension between what we know is God's will and the pull of our own.

Luke tells us that it was the Spirit who led Jesus into the wilderness. Mark, the oldest of the Gospels, uses a much more forceful image when he writes, "The Spirit immediately *drove* him out into the wilderness." While it may not be for the purpose of testing our mettle, I am convinced that the Spirit also puts us in places where our faith and our obedience are sorely challenged, and where we, too, must decide who we will follow. Sometimes we choose these wilderness experiences, such as when we befriend one whom we know will be a "high maintenance" friend because he or she has significant needs, or when we choose to enter into the struggle—emotional, mental, or professional—of another when we could just as easily walk the other way. But sometimes you are chosen for it. You're simply in the wrong place at the right time, or more correctly God's time, and you know God put you there for a reason. I've been there more than once, and I imagine that you have been also. They were not particularly places I would have chosen to go, and had I known the challenge at the beginning, I may well never have accepted it, but there I was, just as you have been, in the right place in God's time. Kathleen Norris writes: "It is never an easy thing to be chosen of God; it is not something people choose for themselves. For Abraham and Sarah, Moses, Jacob, Ruth, Jeremiah, Isaiah, Mary and Jesus himself being God's chosen does not mean doing well. It does not guarantee access to all the answers but means contending with hard questions, thankless tasks, and usually a harrowing journey, which in Jesus' case leads to the cross."[6]

I would be lying to you if I did not admit that I have turned my back on the wilderness on more than one occasion by sidestepping issues that I did not want to address or by not engaging with circumstances and people that I knew would require more of me than I felt I could or wanted to give. I would be lying to you if I told you that I emerged from the wilderness each time with my faith intact and both a better disciple and a better person. Sometimes I have; sometimes I have not. I still bear scars from some of the wounds inflicted

---

[6] Kathleen Norris, *Amazing Grace ~ A Vocabulary of Faith*, (River Head Books, 1999), 140, 141

along the way, and I still struggle with forgiving some of those who inflicted those wounds with apparent delight. Choose them or not, as human beings and as disciples of Jesus Christ, you and I both will know times when we struggle with the choice of following God's will or our own for our lives. The pattern for dealing with that, I think, was set for us by Jesus.

First, Jesus did not turn away from the wilderness but embraced it. Second, Jesus engaged the struggle, which in this case meant being honest about the feelings in his own heart and soul: his fear of want; his desire to sidestep difficulty by giving the people what they wanted—a political savior, and the temptation to utilize his power to effect dramatic things to attract a quick and easy following. Third, Jesus resisted these temptations by falling back upon the scripture written within his heart and soul, and Jesus prayed that he might be strengthened in the face of temptation and be able to commit himself fully to the Father's will for his life. Each time, Jesus chose to follow God's way for him. This turned out to be a far more challenging and costly way than the alternatives.

Remember this, friends, if you don't remember anything else this morning. Whenever you find yourself in the wilderness, embrace it. Be honest with God about your struggle; find direction in God's word in scripture; pray to the Father for strength to obey and know that you are not alone. Jesus is with you in the power of his Spirit to sustain you, to comfort you, to enable you to persevere, and in time to deliver you. And remember this, too. Not only is the Lord with you; your brothers and sisters in the Lord will be with you, if you allow them in. You are surrounded by people who love you, who care for you, and who will walk with you through the darkness into the light.

"A wandering Aramean was my father," but it was the Lord who led him, as it is the Lord who leads you and me. Let us, then, follow with confident faith and obedience.

The Kingdom of God Is Like . . .
Mark 4:26-34

He also said, 'The kingdom of God is as if someone would scatter seed on the ground, and would sleep and rise night and day, and the seed would sprout and grow, he does not know how. The earth produces of itself, first the stalk, then the head, then the full grain in the head. But when the grain is ripe, at once he goes in with his sickle, because the harvest has come.'

He also said, 'With what can we compare the kingdom of God, or what parable will we use for it? It is like a mustard seed, which, when sown upon the ground, is the smallest of all the seeds on earth; yet when it is sown it grows up and becomes the greatest of all shrubs, and puts forth large branches, so that the birds of the air can make nests in its shade.'

With many such parables he spoke the word to them, as they were able to hear it; he did not speak to them except in parables, but he explained everything in private to his disciples.

What is it like to be in love, to hold your newborn child for the first time, to step out into a new venture in life, to reach the mountain top, to break with an addiction, to be the one left behind? "Well, it's like...." The truth is that some things reach beyond the ability of mere words fully to describe. Only the language of metaphor can begin to give expression to the experience, and even then, it has its limits. Jesus used the language of metaphor when seeking to explain the kingdom of God. "The kingdom of God is as if someone would scatter seed on the ground, and would sleep and rise night and day, and the seed would sprout and grow, he does not know how." The Kingdom of God--God's gracious rule in Jesus Christ--grows in ways beyond our vision, control, and understanding, but it grows. Behind, in, and through the things that we can see, and in ways that we cannot see, God is at work to accomplish his good purpose in the world, and in the minuscule pieces of the world that are our lives.

That assurance had to be an enormous comfort to the early church—a tiny collection of insignificant people with a worldwide vision of what is to be when Jesus comes again and the establishment of God's kingdom on earth is completed. Then all things will be made new. God's will shall be done on earth as it is in heaven—not by force or coercion but by the transformation of the human heart—and "every knee will bend, and every tongue confesses that Jesus Christ is Lord to the glory of God the Father." No more hatred, no more war, no more pain, no more brokenness. It is a bold vision, but is it too bold? Are we just fooling ourselves? Is it little more than wishful thinking by people who know too much of hatred, war, pain, and brokenness? "No," said Jesus, for "the kingdom of God is as if someone would scatter seed on the ground, and would sleep and rise night and day, and the seed would sprout and grow, but he does not know how." Or the kingdom of God "is like a mustard seed, which, when sown upon the ground, is the smallest of all the seeds on earth; yet when it is sown it grows up and becomes the greatest of all shrubs, and puts forth large branches, so that the birds of the air can make nests in its shade." From this small beginning in the first century, against enormous odds, the kingdom of God will prevail.

For me that is a source of great comfort and encouragement, because with age and maturity the balance between the limitations of our own power individually and corporately and the power of evil at work in our world seems tilted more and more in favor of evil. Look at the world in which we live—the violence and racial tension in our city streets; the rampant dishonesty in American life and politics; the violence perpetrated by terrorists at home and abroad; the rise of radical Islam and its culture of death; the decline of the Christian church in western culture and the emergence of a secular spirituality that dismisses what it contemptuously labels as "organized religion" as irrelevant to the modern world—it is enough to make you despair. Closer to home you watch as someone you love makes choices that will only bring him increasing pain in life, or as someone you love struggles with a burden imposed upon her, through no fault of her own, from which there will never be a complete escape. You watch as young people die in the prime of life and as old people whose lives have become a burden and who would welcome death as a good friend continue to linger. Jesus assures us, however, that though the world sometimes looks bound and determined to go to hell and God seems preoccupied with something else, God is still at work for its redemption.

Lutheran liturgical scholar Lawrence Stookey writes: "Holy hiddenness is neither a punishment from God nor a denial of grace to us. It is a gift. Luther it is said, at the end of the afternoon frequently would invite one or more of his coworkers to join him in a time of relaxation. But his excessively conscientious associate, Philip Melanchthon, frequently tried to prevent this on the grounds that 'there is too much work to be doing to reform the church'—to which Luther would reply in exasperation, 'Philip, *God* is at work even while we are drinking beer.' God's hidden labors in our midst should allow us to live faithfully without the stultifying intensity that takes us to the brink of self-idolatry by causing us to believe everything of importance depends on us, and us alone." [7]

Yet we are never merely passive spectators in God's work of redemption, cheering God on from the stands, as it were, but as members of the body of Christ, the Church, we are as Wallace Alston once put it, "active participant[s] in God's unparalleled renovation of the world."[8] The parables Jesus told about the kingdom of God invariably contain some element of human responsibility: someone scatters seed upon the ground, or sows a mustard seed, or discovers a

---

[7] Lawrence Stookey, *Calendar: Christ's Time for the Church*, (Abingdon Press, 2007), 18

[8] Wallace Alston, *Guides to the Reformed Tradition: The Church*, (Westminster John Knox Press, 1984), p. 22

treasure hidden in a field or a pearl of great value and sells everything to possess it. It is through us that the word of the Gospel is made known in the world. We—you and I individually and together as the church—are the instruments of God's reconciling and redeeming work in the world. We are the hands that reach to care, the arms that reach to embrace. We are the living evidence of God's sovereign rule on earth, *us:* the way we live, relate, forgive, love and serve not only those closest to us but even the stranger—perhaps especially the stranger. You touch lives with the love of God in Jesus Christ every day simply by being who you are—a follower of Jesus—and much of the time aren't even aware of this.

There are times when it would be easy to make our peace with the way things are, to accept the fact that the world is simply bound and determined to go to hell, and to grab what we can for ourselves and those we love. And there are times when we teeter on the very edge of despair. What keeps our hope alive is the assurance that like seed sown upon the ground or like a tiny mustard seed, the realm of God's gracious rule has taken root and is growing and bearing fruit in your life and mine, in the lives of those we love the most, and in the life of this world even when we cannot see its evidence.

Brothers and sisters, the best is yet to come, for he has the whole world in his hands—every little piece of it. Thanks be to God.

"Hope"
Jeremiah 33:14-16

The days are surely coming, says the Lord, when I will fulfill the promise I made to the house of Israel and the house of Judah. In those days and at that time I will cause a righteous Branch to spring up for David; and he shall execute justice and righteousness in the land. In those days Judah will be saved and Jerusalem will live in safety. And this is the name by which it will be called: 'The Lord is our righteousness.'

It was my day off and I had slept late. Mary, my wife, had to be at work early, and being the kind and thoughtful person, she is, she let me sleep. I didn't even hear her leave. Later, when I rolled out of bed and groggily made my way to the kitchen for a first cup of coffee, I saw her slippers sitting on the mat in front of the sink, positioned as if she had somehow been lifted straight out of them. Propped against the cabinet in front of them was a small erasable board with this message in her handwriting: "Sorry. You missed the rapture."

There are a variety of views on the second coming of the Lord, some of them teeming with judgment and destruction, some with mercy and grace, and some flatly denying it. While the average Presbyterian may not think much about it at all, each year the lections for the First Sunday of Advent nonetheless remind us that the season is more than a time to prepare for the celebration of the birth of Jesus; it is also a time to renew our anticipation of his coming again at the end of all time to complete the work of redemption and renewal begun in him. This day of the Lord's second advent bears both good news and bad. Israel first understood the Day of the Lord as one of unrelenting judgment against her enemies. Later prophets and experiences brought Israel to the sober realization that they, too, stood under the judgment of God. Indeed, some in the prophet Jeremiah's time wondered if the Day had not already come upon them. Jerusalem had been overrun by the Chaldeans. Corpses littered the city's streets and lanes. Homes and businesses lay devastated. The Temple was in ruins, and the King had been taken into captivity. This was the end—the end of their hopes and dreams, their settled and secure life. Everything they had counted on as solid and secure, every emblem of their national identity, had been obliterated. The Lord, in judgment, had withheld his protecting hand, and the worst, the absolute worst had happened.

Yet in the midst of this god-forsakenness, amid the rubble and death that surrounded them at every turn, came not the "I told you so" that some expected from the Lord, but a startling word of hope for the future. As bad as things were, the Lord promised through the prophet: "I am going to bring recovery and healing. In this place of which you say, 'It is a waste without human beings or animals,' in the towns of Judah and the streets of Jerusalem that are desolate, without inhabitants, human or animal, there shall once more be heard the voice of mirth and the voice of gladness, the voice of the bridegroom and the voice of the bride, the voices of those who sing, as they bring thank offerings to the house of the Lord." What is envisioned is a complete reversal, a totally new beginning. Of course, not everyone believed that, just as not everyone would believe it today. If something is too good to be true, well, then it is. You don't need to go hitching your wagon to that star; it is only going to disappoint you. Yet when our choice is between hope and despair, it is to hope that we cling. Hope is what sustains us; it's what keeps us from being completely overwhelmed when the bottom falls out and the world comes crashing in on us. It is what keeps us going from one day to the next, sometimes one moment to the next. To be sure, some hopes are ephemeral: they may sustain us for a while, but then they fade. Bill Oglesby writes: "The paradox is that hope must die before hope can be born. The crucial moment comes with the death of that hope which had in fact proved to be the means of sustaining, at least for a while, but at length is discovered to be unrealistic. In such a crisis moment there is the possibility of overwhelming despair which ultimately leads to death, or of the birth of that hope which reaches beyond the agonizing longing of the moment to that which is even more satisfying than could have been dreamed." [9] You hope for a cure and the hope itself keeps you going through days, weeks, and months of painful treatment, and beyond that hope is the one born of the peace that passes all

---

[9] William Oglesby, *With Wings as Eagles*, (CLC Press, 1966), 140

understanding that assures you that no matter how things turn out, it will be okay, for both in life and in death you are God's own. You hope for a reconciliation in a broken relationship and that hope sustains you while you are in the midst of the darkest days, and beyond that hope, whether realized or not, is the hope born of the assurance that God has a plan for your future, a future that holds within it new beginnings which you would not previously have been able to see. When things are their darkest, said Jesus, "look up for your redemption is near."

"The days are surely coming," declared the prophet, in the name of the Lord, "when I will fulfill the promise I made to the house of Israel and the house of Judah. In those days and at that time, I will cause a righteous branch to shoot up for David, and he will execute justice and righteousness in the land." Theologically we understand that promise as being fulfilled in Jesus, who came among us to show us the love of God and the life God created us to live and enjoy. Through his death and resurrection, God has shattered the power of sin and evil that keep us separate from God, from one another, and from our best selves. God has reconciled us to himself and to one another in Jesus Christ. In him the Kingdom of God, the sphere of God's gracious rule, has come among us and abides with us yet. That is true, but some days it's hard to find evidence of the Kingdom's presence among us and even within us. The good intentions we never quite seem to realize; the mistakes we continue to make; the harm we inflict on those we most love; the evil that lurks within us and occasionally erupts bringing pain to ourselves and to others; the racial tensions that divide our communities; the violence that stalks our streets; the narcissism of a self-indulgent culture, and the blatant greed that marks our corporate life mask the Kingdom's presence among us. And, of course, there are the persistent challenges of hunger, poverty, injustice, and want that mark too much of human life. It's enough to make you despair, and despair we might, were it not for one hope and one hope alone—the hope that is ours in Jesus Christ and God's promises in him. The worries of this life can at times be all but overwhelming, but the trust that we put in God and God's promises to us in Jesus frees us to live, not in fear and dread, but in hopeful anticipation of what is yet to come.

The dome that rises majestically over this building stands as a silent witness that here gather a people of hope. Here gather a people who refuse to accept the status quo as being how it will always be. Here gather a people who recognize the suffering of the world and who, rather than sitting by in lamentation, feel compelled to address that suffering by feeding the hungry, caring for the poor, clothing the naked, welcoming the stranger, embracing the fallen, striving for peace, seeking justice, and sharing the good news of Jesus Christ with the lost. Here gather a people who work for the realization of the kingdom of God on earth, but who are also fully aware that even our most noble efforts will fall short of what God intends, for what God intends for this world is much more than we can ever accomplish. At a time when it may well have seemed that all was falling apart, John Calvin, our father in the Reformed tradition, penned these words:

> *Our hope is in no other save in Thee;*
> *Our faith is built upon Thy promise free;*
> *Lord, give us peace, and make us calm and sure,*
> *That in Thy strength we evermore endure.*

And so, we may and we do. Amen.

Finding Your Life's Calling
Jeremiah 1:4-10

Now the word of the Lord came to me saying,
'Before I formed you in the womb I knew you,
and before you were born I consecrated you;
I appointed you a prophet to the nations.'
Then I said, 'Ah, Lord God! Truly I do not know how to speak, for
I am only a boy.'
But the Lord said to me,
'Do not say, "I am only a boy";
for you shall go to all to whom I send you,
and you shall speak whatever I command you.
Do not be afraid of them,
for I am with you to deliver you,
says the Lord.'
Then the Lord put out his hand and touched my mouth; and the
Lord said to me,
'Now I have put my words in your mouth.
See, today I appoint you over nations and over kingdoms,
to pluck up and to pull down,
to destroy and to overthrow,
to build and to plant.'

The youthful Jeremiah we encounter in our text for today had no intention of becoming a prophet. He came from a family of priests, and if there had been any assumptions about what direction his life would take, it would have been in that direction. In many respects Jeremiah was ill suited for the prophetic office: young, quiet, perhaps even a bit shy—not exactly a personality consistent with the role of prophet with its up-front, even in-your-face, kind of profile. No, Jeremiah was far better suited for the priesthood. God, though, had other plans for him, plans formed before the youth himself had been formed. "Before I formed you in the womb, I knew you, and before you were born, I consecrated you," said the Lord. "I appointed you a prophet to the nations." It was for this that he had been born. It was to this that he was now being called.

Beyond the circumstances of your birth, whatever they may have been; beyond the hopes and dreams your parents had for you or the mold into which they may have tried to cast you, perhaps even beyond your own aspirations and goals for your life is a purpose anchored in the will of God for you. It is often said that ministers are "called" to ministry, and I, for one, believe that. This is more than a profession that you choose for yourself. It is a work to which you are summoned by God's Spirit. People occasionally ask me: "When did you know that you were called to the ministry?" I honestly cannot say when. It's something that more or less evolved for me. Others recognized gifts and abilities in me and encouraged me to consider whether God might be calling me to this life work. There have been ups and downs along the way, times of questioning, times of doubt, times of struggle, and there have been second thoughts from time to time over the last three plus decades, but again and again it has been confirmed for me: this is what you are; this is what you are called to be about. Ministers, though, do not have a monopoly on "call." Every one of us has a calling, a vocation, which is a part of God's plan for our lives. As someone might ask me, "When did you discover that God was calling you to be a minister," I might also ask you, "When did you realize that God was calling you to be a teacher, or a doctor, a homemaker, a scientist, a social worker, a CPA, an administrator, financial advisor, engineer, groundskeeper, whatever?" You see, one's vocation is more than a profession, more than a way of making a living; it is a way of life through which one's sense of purpose, indeed the purpose to which God has called you, finds expression.

Some of us are fortunate enough to discover early on God's call for our lives. We know what we are supposed to do, give ourselves to it, and never—or at least rarely—look back. Others of us may take more time and even flounder a bit before discovering our vocational calling. Some of us may find ourselves called to several different vocations over a lifetime. I heard recently that it is estimated that members of Generation X might expect to change careers—not just jobs but careers—as many as six times in their span of life. And not all are fortunate enough to earn a living from their calling but work at one job or another to make a living, their avocation being their true calling, and their work merely a means to an end. All too often that is the case for artists, musicians, poets, writers, and others. There are also those who discover their passion, their reason for being, in the volunteer sector working with children, with the mentally ill, in the arts, in historic preservation, in ministry to those who struggle with addictions, in efforts to protect the environment, in care for the homeless and hungry, in education efforts with the illiterate—the list goes on and on. Many of you in this sanctuary this morning have retired from successful careers in business, law, finance, medicine, education, or whatever, and have discovered, or were called to related or altogether new ventures in retirement.

For us as Christians vocational choice is shaped not merely by aptitude and desire or by what may be most lucrative, but by our understanding of God's will and purpose for our lives. Our lives, we know, are not merely our own, a possession to be held close and protected, but a trust to be invested and shared. What we do with them matters not merely to us, but to the One who has imparted this gift of life and the interests, skills, and abilities that fill it. God has a purpose for all of us in life, and it is in finding that purpose and pursuing it that we become most authentically the people God created us to be.

Faithfulness in that calling, however, does not always result in the satisfaction and smooth sailing we might expect. Often, most often, it does, but there are those other times. . . . Jesus knew about them. The virulent response of his friends and neighbors to his teaching in the synagogue in Nazareth is proof of that, perhaps the first proof to Jesus of the costly nature of his vocation. Jeremiah knew about those days as well, not so much because of people's violent response to his teaching but because of the public ridicule to which he was subjected. It became such a burden that at more than one point in his journey he lamented ever having answer God's call, indeed ever having been born. "Cursed be the day on which I was born! The day when my mother bore me, let it not be blessed!" he mourned. "Cursed be the man who brought the news to my father, saying, 'A child is born to you, a son,' making him glad. Let that man be like the cities that the Lord overthrew without pity; let him hear a cry in the morning and an alarm at noon, because he did not kill me in the womb; so my mother would have been my grave, and her womb forever great. Why did I come forth from the womb to see toil and sorrow and spend my days in shame?" (20:14-18)

Kathleen Norris writes of a time in her life when she struggled with the cost of faithfulness in her own vocation: "All of us, I suspect, have times when we're made to suffer simply for being who and what we are, and we become adept at inventing means of escape . . . But Jeremiah reminded me that the pain that comes from one's identity, that grows out of the response to call, can't be escaped or pushed aside. It must be gone through. He led me into the heart of pain, forcing me to recognize that to answer a call as a prophet, or a poet for that matter, is to reject the authority of credentials, of human valuation of any kind, accepting only the authority of the call itself. It was as a writer that Jeremiah spoke to me, and it was as a writer that I listened. I couldn't have asked for a better companion."[10]

The way to fulfillment, to satisfaction in life, is not in making those your goals and setting your sights on them, but in discovering through prayer, self-assessment, conversation with others, and reliance upon the Holy Spirit's work in you God's will and purpose for your life, and giving yourself to it. That can be daunting, even overwhelming, and there may well be times when you think to yourself, "Whatever made me think that I could do this?" or "If I had known what it was going to be like . . ." or "Why me, Lord, and not someone else?" But the Lord promises us, as he did a young Jeremiah who objected to God's call in his life, "I will be with you." I *will* be with you.

Wherever you may be in your journey of life—just starting out with the future stretching endlessly before you; in mid-life recognizing that there may well be fewer years before you than behind you, or at that place where you can look back over the decades and see what you could not see before—pause for a moment and consider, just consider, "Am I doing with this gift of life what God in Christ calls me to do?" Think about that.

---

[10] Kathleen Norris, *The Cloister Walk*, (Riverhead Books, 1997), 38

Snap Judgements
John 1:43-51

The next day Jesus decided to go to Galilee. He found Philip and said to him, 'Follow me.' Now Philip was from Bethsaida, the city of Andrew and Peter. Philip found Nathanael and said to him, 'We have found him about whom Moses in the law and also the prophets wrote, Jesus son of Joseph from Nazareth.' Nathanael said to him, 'Can anything good come out of Nazareth?' Philip said to him, 'Come and see.' When Jesus saw Nathanael coming towards him, he said of him, 'Here is truly an Israelite in whom there is no deceit!' Nathanael asked him, 'Where did you come to know me?' Jesus answered, 'I saw you under the fig tree before Philip called you.' Nathanael replied, 'Rabbi, you are the Son of God! You are the King of Israel!' Jesus answered, 'Do you believe because I told you that I saw you under the fig tree? You will see greater things than these.' And he said to him, 'Very truly, I tell you, you will see heaven opened and the angels of God ascending and descending upon the Son of Man.'

I've only had a few experiences in my life in which I have felt the undeniable sting of prejudice or the pain of injustice. I know I should count myself fortunate for that because it isn't the case for some people or groups in our culture, but the memories continue to linger years afterwards. When we lived in another part of the country, I was astounded to discover that some people who considered themselves enlightened progressives reasoned that because I am a white, Southern male with a somewhat large physical presence, then I must also be a homophobic, misogynistic and racist bigot. They could not have been more wrong but trying to tell them that was a waste of time, energy, and breath.

Nathanael reasoned much the same way when it came to this man of whom his friend Philip declared, "We have found him about whom Moses in the law and also the prophets wrote, Jesus son of Joseph from Nazareth." And Nathanael answered, "Can anything good come out of Nazareth." I know that place and believe me—that is not at all the kind of place from which God's anointed one could possibly come. To which Philip answered, "Come and see." Judge for yourself. No amount of arguing, no amount of additional information was going to change Nathanael's mind. "Come and see," and not only his mind but his life was radically changed. He came face to face with one who somehow knew him, really knew him, not merely about him, but his very self. And with Philip, he followed Jesus.

The invitation was to follow, not to walk alongside Jesus, but to follow in his footsteps. I got hearing aids for the first time a couple of months ago, and while the set I got doesn't have a lot of bells and whistles, it does have a fancy little remote that I can use to shift between two settings. When I push the button, there is a lovely female voice that says either "Comfort" or "Master." I prefer the "comfort setting" to the "master." I think the same might be said about following Jesus. There is great comfort in walking with him.

I can assure you that there are parts of the journey of life that I'm not sure I could survive apart from the presence and comfort of the Lord. His peace, his sustaining grace, his abiding love, his forgiveness keeps me going. But Jesus is not merely my comfort and your comfort; he is also the master. We do not so much walk *beside* Jesus as we do *behind* him. That is a rather novel idea in much of American religious thought. Religion is all about me, the culture tells us. It's supposed to make you feel good, enhance your sense of well-being, make your life more fulfilling, and if it doesn't, then find one that suits you and your needs.

In a tongue-in-cheek, one-act play entitled "The McJesus Drama," a variety of customers pull up to a drive-through window to place their "have it your way" orders. One asks for a "Sugar Daddy Jesus." Another orders a "Warm and Fuzzy Jesus." One wants a "Condemning Jesus #5 with extra lightning bolts," and another pulls to the window and says, I would like to buy three dollars' worth of Jesus, please. Not enough to make me a fanatic or drastically alter my lifestyle but just enough to make me feel comfortable. I don't want enough of him to make me love someone with AIDS or become a missionary or anything. Just give me a pound of the supernatural in a paper sack."[11] When we follow Jesus, though, it is on his terms and not ours. We walk behind him, in his steps, not ahead of him, leading the way. That's the very meaning of discipleship.

---

[11] Copyright © 1995, Matthew Pole

The older I have gotten, the more I have come to realize that what matters most in our Christian life is not the orthodoxy of one's belief, but the practice of one's life. Of course, you would hope that those who hold to some measure of orthodoxy would show it in their lives, but that is not always the case. Jesus didn't give the Twelve a test to examine what they believed; he simply called them to follow him. Christian history is full of the examples of saints and martyrs who have done just that, sometimes at great cost to themselves. Patrick Hamilton, George Wishart, John Knox and others from our Scottish Presbyterian heritage suffered for the sake of following Jesus in seeking the Reformation of the church in light of the teachings of the Bible. Martin Luther King, Jr. and others at the forefront of the Civil Rights movement paid the price of following Jesus as they stood up to verbal and physical abuse, faced angry crowds and water cannon, and endured arrest and incarceration as they sought the fuller realization of the kingdom of God in human society through the fair and equitable treatment of people long denied a place at the table.

You don't have to change the world to follow Jesus; only do that which you believe he has called you to do—to live as he lived, to love as he loved, to forgive as he forgave, to accept people as he accepted them. We are called to follow Jesus not merely in a general way, but sometimes in very specific ways. It may be a matter of befriending someone who is lonely or difficult; it may be standing up to an injustice in the community or even in the church; it may be reaching out to a particular person in a particular time of need because you have been where she is. It may be any number of things. It isn't always easy; it can be challenging; it can even be costly. Occasionally I wish Jesus were a little more moderate in his expectations, a little more reasonable. Sometimes I wish Jesus would follow my lead rather than always demanding that I follow his. The truth is that there are some valleys through which I would just as soon not pass and some mountains that I would much rather not climb. I've been there already; done that; and have the tee-shirt to prove it. "Can't we just enjoy the journey?" I sometimes want to say. Ironically, though, what we discover is that it is in following Jesus—wherever that may take us—that we find the life for which we yearn. As St. Francis reminds us: "It is in giving that we receive, it is in pardoning that we are pardoned, and it is in dying that we are born to eternal life." This I will promise you, though: Jesus will never walk off and leave you. Whatever it is that you are called to do in following him, he will be there with you.

"Come and see; judge for yourself," Philip encouraged his friend. And what we discover, as did Nathanael, is one who knows us, really knows us, loves us as we are, and calls us to walk with him in the journey of life. It's a choice that each of us makes, not merely once upon a time, but again and again in the journey of Christian life and discipleship. And it is an invitation that each of us is graced to extend.

Impossible, Simply Impossible
John 6:1-14

After this Jesus went to the other side of the Sea of Galilee, also called the Sea of Tiberias. A large crowd kept following him, because they saw the signs that he was doing for the sick. Jesus went up the mountain and sat down there with his disciples. Now the Passover, the festival of the Jews, was near. When he looked up and saw a large crowd coming towards him, Jesus said to Philip, 'Where are we to buy bread for these people to eat?' He said this to test him, for he himself knew what he was going to do. Philip answered him, 'Six months' wages would not buy enough bread for each of them to get a little.' One of his disciples, Andrew, Simon Peter's brother, said to him, 'There is a boy here who has five barley loaves and two fish. But what are they among so many people?' Jesus said, 'Make the people sit down.' Now there was a great deal of grass in the place; so they sat down, about five thousand in all. Then Jesus took the loaves, and when he had given thanks, he distributed them to those who were seated; so also the fish, as much as they wanted. When they were satisfied, he told his disciples, 'Gather up the fragments left over, so that nothing may be lost.' So they gathered them up, and from the fragments of the five barley loaves, left by those who had eaten, they filled twelve baskets. When the people saw the sign that he had done, they began to say, 'This is indeed the prophet who is to come into the world.'

He looked down into their hopeful faces from the mountainside. They had followed him from the other side of the lake because they had seen the "signs of what he was doing for the sick." And I imagine that they brought their sick with them. The infirm and dying they bore on makeshift gurneys; the blind they led by the hand. They supported the crippled, and children too weak to walk they carried in their arms. Some of their infirmities were obvious, but others were not evident to the eye: mental and spiritual illness, brokenness of spirit, sorrow, guilt, and a host of other maladies to which we ourselves are no strangers. They brought those to Jesus as well. Around him gathered a sea of hopeful humanity.

Jesus was aware of all that, but he also recognized a much more pressing need. Having followed him such a great distance, if they weren't already hungry, they soon would be, and no one can listen, really listen, even to good news, if he is hungry. Knowing already what he was going to do, Jesus nonetheless turned to Philip, one of the Twelve, and asked: "Where are we to buy bread for these people to eat?" In answering him Philip did not bother with the question of where a sufficient quantity of bread might be found, for even if it could be found he knew that there was no way that they could afford to buy it. "Six months' wages would not buy enough bread for each of them to get a little," he told Jesus. It simply could not be done. The cost would be prohibitive. Andrew, who had heard this exchange, offered that he had seen "a boy here who has five barley loaves and two fish," but he quickly added: "What are they among so many people?" Both Philip and Andrew faced the fact that Jesus himself should have clearly seen: what he was asking was impossible. Much as they would like to do something, there really was nothing they could do.

All of us, I imagine, at one time or another, have stood where Philip and Andrew stood, and some of us may stand there today. Before us are opportunities which we really would like to pursue; needs we long to supply; wrongs we yearn to right, but taking stock of the resources at hand and measuring the challenges before us, we conclude, not at all unreasonably, that the challenge or need far exceeds what we have to bring, and so, much as we might want, there really isn't anything that we can do. Kennon Callahan, in one of his books, used the analogy of an athletic team taking the field to describe our response to particular challenges in our lives, in the life of the church and in the life of the world. Some teams, he said, play to win. Each team member brings the full measure of his strength, energy, discipline and athletic ability to the game, and playing as one they set out not only to win, but to excel in winning. Others, says Callahan, play to avoid losing, like a student content with making just passing grades. Squeaking by is good enough. Some teams, for whatever reason, play to lose. They believe the game is lost before they ever take the field. And finally, there are those who simply refuse to leave the locker room. Andrew and Philip fall into that category. Why try? You can't buy what you don't have the money to buy, and you can't share what you don't have to share.

We live in a world that is growing smaller and smaller. Global problems are increasingly becoming local problems. Hatred and its violence strike ever closer to home. Just in this month we have seen the deaths of nine worshipers in Charleston, SC, the murders of four unarmed military personnel as they went about their duties in Chattanooga, TN, and the murder of two people and the injuring of nine others by a "drifter" in a movie theater in Lafayette, LA. Racial hatred, militant religious fanaticism, and pure evil lie at the root of these and other acts of violence. Surely there must be something that we can do. But what? While some argue that the answer is more stringent gun control, others insist with equal vehemence that this is not the answer. Some celebrate the nuclear treaty with Iran as an international breakthrough of historic proportions; others see it as the worst international agreement since Neville Chamberlain's "peace in our time" treaty with Adolph Hitler. Some lament the systematic killing of Christians at the hands of ISIS, while others try to temper that reality by pointing out that others are being killed, too. Many among us bemoan the loss of a sense of responsibility and accountability in our culture; we are shocked by the decline in moral values and the narcissism that characterizes much of modern life. Some of us in ecclesiastical leadership, while perhaps not lamenting the demise of Christendom, do lament the loss of the church's influence on the moral values of the secular culture and the decline in church membership and attendance. We look at the world around us; the struggles in our communities and, the challenges in our own lives and sometimes wonder: "What can we do?" Even our best efforts seem puny and ineffective in the face of such enormous challenges. Why even leave the locker room? In the context of our reading from John, it would be like trying to whip up a meal for 5,000 plus with only a couple of bucks in your pocket and at a moment's notice.

It is important to remember that what Jesus asked Philip and Andrew was not: "Where will *you* find bread for these people to eat?" but where will *we*? I suppose Jesus could have satisfied the hunger of the people that day quite on his own, if he had chosen, but that is not how Jesus chooses to work. He took what was at hand, what was offered, gave thanks for it and with it fed a multitude. What may seem to you and me as little more than a pittance can in the hands of Jesus be multiplied a thousand-fold and more. Don't ever think you have nothing to offer; don't ever think that there isn't anything that you can do. Everyone has something, and everyone can do something. The boy offered what he had—the best of what he had—to Jesus to meet the need at hand. That is how Jesus chooses to work—through you and me and the gifts we have to offer. Whatever may be the gift you have to bring to the challenge or need at hand, though it may seem a pittance to you, if it is the best that you have to bring, bring it, place it in the hands of Jesus, and along with it your hand as well, and trust him not only to make it adequate for the task at hand but abundantly sufficient.

Neither you nor I is responsible or capable of fully realizing the Kingdom of God. That is God's business, and it is God, sometimes through us, sometimes despite us, and very often far beyond us in ways we cannot begin to understand, who will fully establish his rule so that his will is done on earth as it is in heaven. Do what you can do, the best that you can do, and leave the rest in the hands of God.

Bread of Life
John 6:24-35

So when the crowd saw that neither Jesus nor his disciples were there, they themselves got into the boats and went to Capernaum looking for Jesus.

When they found him on the other side of the lake, they said to him, 'Rabbi, when did you come here?' Jesus answered them, 'Very truly, I tell you, you are looking for me, not because you saw signs, but because you ate your fill of the loaves. Do not work for the food that perishes, but for the food that endures for eternal life, which the Son of Man will give you. For it is on him that God the Father has set his seal.' Then they said to him, 'What must we do to perform the works of God?' Jesus answered them, 'This is the work of God, that you believe in him whom he has sent.' So they said to him, 'What sign are you going to give us then, so that we may see it and believe you? What work are you performing? Our ancestors ate the manna in the wilderness; as it is written, "He gave them bread from heaven to eat." ' Then Jesus said to them, 'Very truly, I tell you, it was not Moses who gave you the bread from heaven, but it is my Father who gives you the true bread from heaven. For the bread of God is that which comes down from heaven and gives life to the world.' They said to him, 'Sir, give us this bread always.'

Jesus said to them, 'I am the bread of life. Whoever comes to me will never be hungry, and whoever believes in me will never be thirsty.

One of the images of my father that I have carried with me from childhood is of him standing in front of the refrigerator, left arm drooped over the top of the open door, his body bent at the waist so that he could clearly see the inside, and asking of no one in particular: "Do we have anything to eat?" We *always* had something to eat, but the question from this man who had known the pangs of hunger in his childhood was more accurately, "Do we have anything to eat that I *want*?"

Hunger is something of which few, if any of us gathered here, have any firsthand knowledge. We may know what it is like to be out of the food that we want to eat at the moment; we may know the growling of an empty stomach while we wait for the next meal or snack, but few, if any of us, know what it means to go without. The crowd following Jesus from one side of the lake to the other knew that well. These were people for whom hunger was a part of the rhythm of daily life—farmers who knew both feast and famine; day workers who lived hand to mouth, mothers who would forego food for themselves so that their children might eat. These people followed Jesus on this occasion for no other reason than that he had given them bread and fish, and not just a little, but "as much as they wanted," which was a novelty for them. Jesus understood that. "You seek me not because you saw signs, but because you ate your fill of the loaves," he told them, not so much as a rebuke, but as a simple statement of fact. He knew it was not his teaching, not even the miracles of healing that were had at his hands, that attracted the crowd, but something far more fundamental, something as basic to human life as food. Jesus wanted to give them something more than bread and fish. He wanted to give them that food which satisfies the gnawing emptiness of the human spirit. "Do not labor for the food which perishes," he admonished them, "but for the food that endures for eternal life, which the Son of man will give you." "Lord, give us this bread always," they implored.

Knowing what you want out of life is half the battle. For some people the choices are few, but for us they are many, and that may be part of our problem. Before us is a banquet table laden with delicious offerings, each promising to make our lives complete. What do you want? What do you think will satisfy you? We live in a culture of discontent that sends us back to the table again and again in search of that one more thing that will bring it all together. The culture puts us on trial and judges us lacking. Your teeth are too dull, your hair is lifeless, you're too fat, too thin, too bald, too gray, too tall, too short, too boring, too impetuous. If you had more money, less stress, a different job, a taller steeple . . . Whatever may be the need, you can buy it, you can achieve it, you can win it, we are told—but what you and I *aren't* told is that no matter how much you have it will never be enough. If some is good, more must be better, and the more you have, the more you think you need. It is an endless, self-defeating cycle. You and I may pile our plates high with the offerings before us—and we are certainly encouraged to do just that—but no matter how delicious, how inviting, how beautiful they may be, none can satisfy the deepest longing of the human spirit, which in John's Gospel is called "eternal life."

"We think of Eternal Life, if we think of it at all," writes Frederick Buechner, "as what happens when life ends. We would do better to think of it as what happens when life begins. St. Paul uses the phrase . . . to describe the end and goal of the process of salvation. Elsewhere he writes the same thing in a remarkable sentence where he says that the whole purpose of God's slogging around through the muck of history and of our own individual histories is somehow to prod us, jolly us, worry us, cajole us, and if need be bludgeon us into reaching 'maturity, to the measure of the full stature of Christ.' (Ephesians 4:13) In other words, to live Eternal Life in the full and final sense is to be with God as Christ is with him, and with each other as Christ is with us."[12] Yet, our experience of eternal life in this life is both fleeting and fragmentary. Still, we know it. We know it in the peace that passes all understanding—you know, that peace that wells within you when everything around you is wracked by confusion, uncertainty, and struggle, and you have no rational reason to feel at peace. Eternal life is what you experience when joy rises unexpectedly from somewhere deep within your soul and you find yourself "lost in wonder, love and praise." Eternal life is what you experience when you can forgive, honestly forgive,

---

[12] Frederick Buechner, *Wishful Thinking: A Theological ABC*, (Harper and Row, Publishers, Inc. New York, NY 1973), 22-23

someone you never thought you could. Eternal life is that fleeting moment of unexpected clarity when all the disparate parts of your life come together as one, and it all makes sense, and you know everything is right, just *right*. Eternal life is what you experience when you know, I mean really *know*, that God is real because you can feel God's presence beside you and see the evidence of his sustaining, saving, and loving hand in your life.

"What must we do?" the eager crowd asked him. We always think that there is something that we *must* do, and the truth is that sometimes that would be easier. Do this one thing or these several things and your life will be complete. "In it to win it," was the sermon title on the sign in front of a church I passed on my way here this morning. But it doesn't work that way. No matter how good you might be; no matter how much you might accomplish; no matter how much you give away, it will never be enough. When the people asked him, "What must we do to perform the works of God?" Jesus said to them, "This is the work of God, that you believe in him whom he has sent." Belief implies more than assent to an intellectual proposition or body of knowledge; here it means trust. Christianity is more than a set of principles or a commitment to compassion, justice, and peace. It is based upon a relationship, the relationship we share with God in Jesus Christ. It is in knowing God and wanting to be known by him. "I am the bread of life," Jesus said. "Whoever comes to me will never be hungry, and whoever believes in me will never be thirsty." The banquet table set before us in this world is overflowing with tasty and enticing alternatives, like the fruit of the knowledge of good and evil in the Garden, but none of them or even all of them together can ever satisfy the deepest longing of the human soul, for that longing is nothing less than the longing to be, once again, united with him who made us and declared us good. As St. Augustine put it, "Our souls are restless till they find their rest in Thee."

Now I'm not about to tell you that when you believe in Jesus, all the questions will be answered, the longing in the depths of your being will be fully satisfied, and life will be completely as God means for it to be for you. What I *will* tell you and what I believe from the very depths of my being is that the food and drink that will sustain the life of the spirit—the eternal life of the Scriptures—is found in Jesus Christ alone. Like the food and drink we need to sustain our physical bodies, we continue to need to eat and drink of him who is the bread of life and the cup of salvation, not once upon a time, but again and again in the walk of human life as we reflect upon the witness of scripture; as we make time simply to kneel quietly in the presence of the Lord; as we give ourselves to works of mercy and grace; as we share together in corporate worship, and especially as we gather at this table to break the bread and to share the cup of eternal life. The table is set; the feast is ready. Come, let us lift up the cup of salvation and call on the name of the Lord.

Jumping Ship
John 6:56-59

Those who eat my flesh and drink my blood abide in me, and I in them. Just as the living Father sent me, and I live because of the Father, so whoever eats me will live because of me. This is the bread that came down from heaven, not like that which your ancestors ate, and they died. But the one who eats this bread will live forever.' He said these things while he was teaching in the synagogue at Capernaum.

Have you ever just wanted to walk away from it all? I imagine most of us have at some time or another in our lives. Some of us have done precisely that, if for no other reason than to preserve some semblance of sanity. While others of us have stood our ground in the hope that somehow, someday, things would turn around. Maybe they did, but then again, maybe you're still waiting. Whatever the case, the contradiction between how we think things will be and the way they turn out can present us with some of the more significant moral, ethical, and spiritual dilemmas of our lives.

That was the case for the followers of Jesus in our reading from the Gospel of John. Initially drawn to him and his message, they were now turning away, not merely one or two here and there, but in numbers large enough that Jesus turned to the Twelve, the trusted inner circle, and asked, "Do you wish to go away also?" Those who were leaving complained, "This is a hard saying. Who can listen to it?" The immediate context of the complaint was the Lord's assertion, "Very truly I tell you, *unless* you eat the flesh of the Son of Man and drink his blood, you have no life in you. Those who eat my flesh and drink my blood have eternal life, and I will raise them up at the last day." (John 6:53, 54) The language is, to say the least, off-putting, but it was more than the graphic nature of the language that prompted them to walk away. It was the depth of the demand that Jesus made of them. "It is the spirit that gives life," he told them; "the flesh is useless." When Jesus spoke of the "flesh," he was referring not to the physical nature of human life—this flesh and blood—but to an outlook, a perspective, a particular worldview. The "flesh" is all that the world values as truly important and which the world touts as being the means to the ultimate treasure, the key to human freedom and fulfillment. Jesus called upon them to choose. Who will be God to you? Who will shape your life, your values, your goals, your conduct, your priorities? Who or what will give your life meaning and purpose? And they voted with their feet.

The Gospel or good news about Jesus both attracts and repels. It attracts because it speaks to our deepest human need. It offers a sense of assurance in the face of life's struggles and disappointments; a promise of forgiveness and freedom from burdens of guilt that weigh us down; the gift of peace in the midst of turmoil, of joy in the midst of sadness, of meaning in a world of fleeting promises, of hope in the face of despair, and life in the grip of death. And yet the Gospel also repels because it holds up as inadequate the food we have sought and continue to seek to satisfy the hunger within us. "It is the spirit that gives life; the flesh is useless." The "flesh" offers up a veritable smorgasbord of delectable and enticing dishes into which we are invited to sink our teeth: power, wealth, fame, sex, and drugs among them, but common to all of them is the idolization of the self. What do *I* want out of life? What will satisfy *my* desires? What will work best for *me*? What will fit *my* lifestyle; what will make *me* feel good? A diet of that, said Jesus, will starve you to death.

Jesus invites us to relinquish the junk food diet that has been our daily bread, and to feed upon the bread of life. To partake of that bread, which is Jesus, is to recognize that the "flesh" is not an end, and *that* is in a sense to die—to die to all the presuppositions about life that we have inherited from the world around us. It is to die to the pride of power that the world holds so dear, to the pride of class or race or economic or intellectual status that prompts us to think of others as somehow less than ourselves. It is to die to the standards of greatness and success by which the world values human life. The Gospel of Jesus demands from us a moral response that involves not simply the affirmation of our minds and the love of our hearts, but the ongoing refocusing of our vision, the reordering of our priorities, the reformulating of our values, indeed the surrender of our lives to be remade after the image of Christ. Jesus calls for nothing less than a complete reversal of human values, a radical reorientation of life as we know it and live it.

It is no wonder that those who initially heard Jesus speak of the bread that gives life and who implored him, "Lord, give us this bread always," had begun to drift away when they heard more about what Jesus really meant. "This is a hard saying; who can listen to it?" they complained. Or, as another translation puts it, "This is more than we can stomach; why listen to it?" We can understand that, I think, for while we may not want to chuck it all and walk away from Jesus as those folks did, we do find ourselves doing less than Jesus demands, because what Jesus demands is sometimes difficult and challenging. He leads us into places and circumstances where we would rather not go. He calls us to tasks that we might rather not do. He presents us with moral and ethical questions that require us to struggle with questions of right and wrong. I don't mean to infer that it is always this way; it isn't, not by a long shot. However, when it is, the struggle between faithfulness and faithlessness, obedience and disobedience can be, and often is intense.

"Do you wish to go away, too?" Jesus asked the Twelve as the crowd thinned. Sometimes, if we are truthful, we must answer yes. The cost of discipleship is higher than we may have first imagined and higher than we may want to pay. Yet Peter's words are our words also: "Lord, to whom shall we go? You have the words of eternal life." Those words were for Peter and they are for us not so much an expression of resignation as of hope, for we know, deep within our beings, that in Jesus is the life for which we long: life that is full, free, and eternal. Indeed, in Jesus that life is taking form in us day by day, moment by moment. "Lord, give us this bread always." Even when it may be hard to swallow, "Lord, give us this bread always.

A Listening Presence
Mark 5:21-34

When Jesus had crossed again in the boat to the other side, a great crowd gathered round him; and he was by the lake. Then one of the leaders of the synagogue named Jairus came and, when he saw him, fell at his feet and begged him repeatedly, 'My little daughter is at the point of death. Come and lay your hands on her, so that she may be made well, and live.' So he went with him. And a large crowd followed him and pressed in on him. Now there was a woman who had been suffering from hemorrhages for twelve years. She had endured much under many physicians and had spent all that she had; and she was no better, but rather grew worse. She had heard about Jesus and came up behind him in the crowd and touched his cloak, for she said, 'If I but touch his clothes, I will be made well.' Immediately her hemorrhage stopped; and she felt in her body that she was healed of her disease. Immediately aware that power had gone forth from him, Jesus turned about in the crowd and said, 'Who touched my clothes?' And his disciples said to him, 'You see the crowd pressing in on you; how can you say, "Who touched me?"' He looked all round to see who had done it. But the woman, knowing what had happened to her, came in fear and trembling, fell down before him, and told him the whole truth. He said to her, 'Daughter, your faith has made you well; go in peace and be healed of your disease.'

She had become more and more an invisible person, this woman hiding in the crowd. She had grown accustomed to her life of solitude, the distance of others, and, for the most part, understood their standoffishness. Her medical condition had made her ritually unclean, and anyone serious about their religious life and wanting to maintain their place in the community found it necessary to stand apart from her. Her friends had wandered away long before, and those who would befriend her—come close enough to touch her, to hold her in one of those times when she thought for sure she was dying—if there were any at all, were few and far between. Sympathy or pity she might receive, but always from a safe distance. She wearied of her illness, its discomfort and embarrassment. She longed to be made well, and had bankrupted herself in search of a cure, but she might as well have been throwing her money down a dry well.

Just being there that day was risky, but the crowd was large, and their attention was directed at the rabbi named Jesus, whom they had all come out to see. It was said that with a word he had stilled a life-threatening storm at sea. It was said that at his command a host of demons had been exorcised from a man who lived across the lake, and it was said with confidence that he had healed many people with a variety of ailments, and so she had made up her mind to be there that day. She wouldn't ask anything of him, but if she could only get close enough to touch him, even the hem of his garment, she was sure that she would be made well. Her heart sank, though, when the crowd parted to allow one of the rulers of the synagogue access to Jesus. The man was clearly distressed. Falling before Jesus in the sand along the shore, he begged not once, but repeatedly: "My little daughter is at the point of death. Come and lay your hands on her, so that she may be made well and live." As Jesus and the man walked away, the woman realized that this might be her last chance. Squeezing through the crowd and drawing as close as she dared, she stretched out her arm, and the tips of her fingers brushed lightly across the hem of his garment. She felt it immediately--the surge of healing within her body.

Jesus felt it, too, and demanded: "Who touched my clothes?" "Who cares," thought Jairus, whose daughter lay dying. "Let's keep moving. There is no time to waste. Every second matters." But Jesus stopped and waited, just waited for whoever it was who had touched him to answer. "In fear and trembling," Mark tells us, the woman "fell down before him, and told him the whole truth." I imagine that what came out of her mouth was more, far more, than simply the story of how she had made her way through the crowd and surreptitiously reached out a hand for healing. I imagine that what she shared with him was the story of her life--how it had been and what it had become because of her illness. I imagine that what she shared with him was her sense of isolation, her numbing loneliness, her shame. And Jesus listened, just listened as if her voice were the only voice in the world and that listening to her was the most important thing he had to do. What Jesus offered the woman—and offers us—is not merely an audience, but a presence. He was there with her; he took time for her; he showed her that she really mattered and that he cared. That is how Jesus cared for people and how Jesus cares for you and me--not simply as one among many in the crowd, but one at a time, listening, really listening to what we are saying, hearing not simply the sound, but the meaning in and between, behind and before the words we speak.

So, he calls us to listen to one another, yet, too often we feel compelled to say something, even though we never are sure what to say. "I'm thinking of you and have you in my prayers. If there is anything, I can do . . ." Very often, though, the words we have to offer sound pathetically empty in the face of the pain or the loss. Spoken in love, they nonetheless sound like a "noisy gong or clanging cymbal." What we sometimes forget is that there are times when listening can be far more important than speaking. Aside from asking "Who touched my clothes?" and the words he spoke when he dismissed her, Jesus said nothing else to the woman in this story from Mark's Gospel. He only listened, listened as "she told him the whole truth." Dietrich Bonhoeffer said, "The first service that one owes to others in the fellowship consists in listening to them. Just as love to God begins with listening to his Word, so the beginning of love for [others in the church] is listening to them. . .. Christians, especially ministers, so often think they must always contribute something when they are in the company of others, that this is the service they have to render. They forget that listening can be a greater service than speaking."[13] He's right, you

---

[13] Dietrich Bonhoeffer, *Life Together*, (Harper and Row, NY, 1954), 97,

know? Too often we feel like we must say something profound or do something to make it better. Otherwise, we haven't helped, but sometimes it is not help that people are looking for—or words of comfort or advice or even answers—but only the gift of a listening presence. That can be difficult sometimes. It isn't always easy to find the time, and with some people, to be honest, we may not want to find the time. They are forever negative and listening to them only brings us down. Some of them like bad news more than good and complaining more than doing something about the issue or issues at hand. There is a point where listening can become enabling, and that does no one any good.

You can't make anyone unburden themselves to you, and you may well not be the person with whom they would choose to do that, but there are those times and those circumstances when for whatever reason, happenstance or providence, you *are* the one. Be aware, listening can be costly. It can cost you some of your time, your emotional energy, and even physical energy. One of my favorite quotes of Henri Nouwen reminds me: "Those who do not run from our pains but touch them with compassion bring healing and new strength. The paradox indeed is that the beginning of healing is in the solidarity with the pain. In our solution-oriented society, it is more important than ever to realize that wanting to alleviate pain without sharing it is like wanting to save a child from a burning house without the risk of being hurt."[14] The gift of a listening presence draws us close, close enough to feel the pain of the other. But it can also be a great blessing, not only to the one who speaks, but to the one who hears. You can't solve other people's problems for them; you can't make it all right, but sometimes in listening, just listening, you can make it better.

---

[14] Henri Nouwen, *Reaching Out*, (Double Day, New York, New York, 1975), 47

Seeing with Clarity
Mark 10:46-52

They came to Jericho. As he and his disciples and a large crowd were leaving Jericho, Bartimaeus son of Timaeus, a blind beggar, was sitting by the roadside. When he heard that it was Jesus of Nazareth, he began to shout out and say, 'Jesus, Son of David, have mercy on me!' Many sternly ordered him to be quiet, but he cried out even more loudly, 'Son of David, have mercy on me!' Jesus stood still and said, 'Call him here.' And they called the blind man, saying to him, 'Take heart; get up, he is calling you.' So throwing off his cloak, he sprang up and came to Jesus. Then Jesus said to him, 'What do you want me to do for you?' The blind man said to him, 'My teacher, let me see again.' Jesus said to him, 'Go; your faith has made you well.' Immediately he regained his sight and followed him on the way.

You do what you have to do sometimes, and that is precisely what this man named Bartimaeus did. Day after day, week after week, this blind man sat there cross-legged in the dust beside the road from Jericho to Jerusalem, calling out at the sound of approaching footsteps and listening for the sound of a coin or a scrap of bread to be tossed in his direction. Mark's Gospel tells us that as Jesus, his disciples, and others composing a large crowd were departing from Jericho for Jerusalem, the blind man, who would have remained pretty much unnoticed had he not called attention to himself, began to cry out, "Jesus, Son of David, have mercy on me!" Here was one, he had heard, who could restore his sight. Many among the crowd admonished him to be quiet, but he called out in an even louder voice, "Jesus, Son of David, have mercy on me!" Imagine the hope of being healed and, along with it, the fear of remaining unnoticed by the roadside. So again and again he called until Jesus took notice of him, stopped, and asked: "What do you want me to do for you?" And without a moment's hesitation the man answered, "My teacher, let me see again."

"What do you want me to do for you?" For some of us, like the blind man, there is no question, no doubt. The crying needs of our lives come rushing forth like water cascading over the falls. "I want healing, Lord, healing for myself, for my child, for my loved one. I want freedom Lord, freedom from the addiction that holds me captive and that is draining the life from me; freedom from the fears that rise within me when I think about the future; freedom from the hurt that throbs within me, freedom from the depression that descends like a dark cloud and all but suffocates me. I want peace, Lord: peace of mind, peace within my family, peace in my community. I want hope, Lord: hope that tomorrow might indeed be better than today, that the future that lies before me holds something more than a repetition of this day's disappointment, struggle, or anxiety.

Others of us, though, while we know what we need, aren't at all sure that we want it. Healing, you see, will bring changes into our lives that we may not want to embrace. Maybe that is why Jesus, rather than simply laying his hands on him and healing the obviously blind man, asked: "What do you want me to do for you?" Perhaps Bartimaeus had become really quite satisfied with the shape of his life, or at least accustomed to it, and had no particular desire to see the light of day. The gift of sight would mark the end of his begging, the end of his life as he knew it. He would have to find another way of supporting himself. The gift of sight would reshape the way people related to him and he related to them. His world would be entirely different.

The truth is that we don't always want to be healed. We have made our peace with the way things are in our lives and cannot imagine life otherwise. We love sickness more than health; the shackles of addiction more than freedom; the burden of guilt more than the gift of forgiveness, fighting the battle more than the gift of peace. The sickness, the addiction, the guilt, the anger, the foe becomes less an enemy and more a friend, a friend apart from whom we cannot imagine our lives. If you are like me, though, it's not any one thing in particular that needs Jesus' healing touch but a number of things at once—fears to be overcome, faults to be corrected, attitudes to be adjusted, habits to be broken, prejudices to be erased, sins to be forgiven. It's sometimes hard to know where to begin, and like Peter at the footwashing on Maundy Thursday what I want to say is, "Lord, not my feet only, but also my hands and my head"—every part of my being, every aspect of my life. That may be what I want to pray, but I am sometimes hesitant, and you are as well, if you are honest about it, because we know that if our request were granted, you and I might well be healed not only in the ways of our expectation, but in ways that we never dreamed we needed.

Inevitably we get more than we bargained for. You see, Jesus is not interested in simply giving you and me a minor tune-up or a modest remodeling. Jesus' desire is to make us whole, and that happens not all at once, but over a lifetime as we grow in knowledge, in grace, and in love. In the early church it was sometimes the custom that those preparing to profess their faith and pass through the waters of baptism would gather at the baptismal pool just at the break of dawn, and, facing the west (the place of the setting sun, symbolic of the darkness of life apart from Christ) renounce sin and its power in the world. Then physically turning to face the east (the place of the rising sun, and symbolic of the light of Christ and new life) they professed their faith in Jesus as Lord and Savior and pledged themselves to live as his faithful disciples. Then they passed through the waters of baptism, from darkness to light, from death to new life. Living out one's baptismal identity, turning from one life—life as it is shaped by this world—to the other—life as it is shaped by the will and purpose of God—goes on for a lifetime. To be sure, we do better some days than others, but whether at a steady pace or one marked by starts and stops, in a straight line or the most circuitous route, it is a journey toward completion, toward becoming the people God created us to be. That happens not merely as the fruit of our own moral and spiritual effort, but also as we give ourselves over to the work of the Holy Spirit in our lives. As we release the grip that we have on our lives, as we relinquish our control and surrender to the work of the Spirit within us, we are changed, changed in ways we never knew we needed or dreamed possible.

"What do you want me to do for you?" The man's need was apparent to anyone with eyes to see, and certainly apparent to Jesus, who knows us even better than we know ourselves. So why ask? Because that is the nature of grace. Grace cannot be imposed upon us; grace cannot be forced upon us or it ceases to be grace. It is simply offered, freely and fully. Still Jesus asks, "What do you want me to do for you?" Think about that; pray about it.

And Taking First Place Is . . .
Mark 9:30-37

They went on from there and passed through Galilee. He did not want anyone to know it; for he was teaching his disciples, saying to them, 'The Son of Man is to be betrayed into human hands, and they will kill him, and three days after being killed, he will rise again.' But they did not understand what he was saying and were afraid to ask him.

Then they came to Capernaum; and when he was in the house, he asked them, 'What were you arguing about on the way?' But they were silent, for on the way they had argued with one another about who was the greatest. He sat down, called the twelve, and said to them, 'Whoever wants to be first must be last of all and servant of all.' Then he took a little child and put it among them; and taking it in his arms, he said to them, 'Whoever welcomes one such child in my name welcomes me, and whoever welcomes me welcomes not me but the one who sent me.'

On their way to Capernaum, Jesus had heard his disciples discussing who among them was the greatest. Peter could have made a convincing argument for himself, I imagine, as could James or John, and if "the Donald" had been among them, there would not have been any doubt, especially in his mind, as to who among them was the greatest. The twelve had not realized that Jesus had heard them, and when he confronted them about it, they were rendered speechless with embarrassment. Still, they were "setting their minds not on divine things but on earthly things," as Jesus had previously rebuked Peter for having done, and their silence indicates they knew precisely how wrong they had been. But, then, rather than chiding them, Jesus carefully explained, "Whoever wants to be first must be last of all and servant of all."

That is about as backwards as you can get, at least by the world's standards. In the world's order of things, greatness is measured in terms of one's achievements, in one's net financial worth, or one's social, political, family, or professional prominence. The first is the winner, not the loser, the one who doesn't get voted off the island or eliminated from the list of contestants. Because of their success, the winners are oftentimes seen as being somehow inherently more valuable than the rest of us. When you are the object of the public's adoration, resisting the temptation to buy into that can be rather challenging, I imagine. We see that all too often in sports figures, screen and stage stars, reality TV performers, politicians, and the super-wealthy who act as though their celebrity status or net worth should somehow exempt them from the standards to which other mere mortals are held. In some ways the public participates in that self-deception by standing ready with excuses for their failures or blatant denial of their wrongdoing.

Who doesn't like to win? Who doesn't like to be affirmed? There is nothing wrong in working hard and succeeding, in being the best or among the best in whatever may be your field of endeavor. It is, in fact, quite commendable and it is to such excellence that we are called. God does not equip us with gifts and abilities so that we may neglect them or squander them in mediocrity. Jesus in no way disparages the desire to excel or to be first; rather, he redefines what that means. In the kingdom of God, the standard by which greatness is measured is not the service one can demand but the service one can render. It is not the pride of place that one can claim, but the humility of one who serves without concern for place. To make his point Jesus took a child into his arms and said, "Whoever welcomes one such child in my name welcomes me and whoever welcomes me welcomes not me but the one who sent me." We bend over backwards for our children and grandchildren, proudly showing off their photos, affirming their successes, and doing all that we can to help them succeed. That was not the case in Jesus' time. A child's place was not at the center of attention, but somewhere on the distant periphery, seen but not heard. As he so often did, Jesus here identifies with the lowest, the weakest, and the most vulnerable among us. By the standards of the kingdom of God, whatever your place in life may be—at the front of the line or the end, at the top of the heap or the bottom, at the pinnacle of success or plugging along somewhere below—doesn't matter. What does matter is the welcome you give to others, especially those who are the weakest, the most vulnerable, the needy.

That is not to say that you must walk in the footsteps of Mother Theresa or forego all the comforts of life to be of the kingdom. It doesn't require a vow of poverty or celibacy or a commitment to missionary life in some foreign country, though it might for you. What such living does entail is, first, an honest self-evaluation which recognizes that no matter what side of the tracks you were born on or on which side you presently live, your life is as valuable, but no more valuable in the eyes of God as any other. We share a common humanity and a common need before God. We share a common grace from God, who sent his Son to live among us, to die for us, and to be raised to life for us all. As it entails an honest self-evaluation, kingdom living also requires an engagement with the weak, the vulnerable, and the needy among us after the example of Jesus. Random acts of kindness and occasional deeds of mercy are nice, but Jesus calls us to something more consistent than that; he calls us to a way of life awake and alert to the world around us and the needs of the people with whom we share the life of the world.

Our minds go immediately to the refugee crisis in Europe and the Middle East; to those who suffer in the aftermath of natural disasters of enormous proportions; to the poor, the homeless, and the hungry in our own community. There are others, too, some of them as close as down the street, next door, within the walls of the church, or even within your own home. They are the sick, the dying, the grieving, the mentally ill and the marginalized among us. They are the parents of the difficult child; the teen struggling with her sexual identity or the kid at school who just doesn't fit in. They are the gay or lesbian couple or Muslim family new to the neighborhood—the people on the outside. You know who they are as well as I do. Jesus said that when you welcome such a one, you welcome not only him but the one who sent him.

That is difficult for us sometimes. The reasons, I imagine, are many. Some of the hurt, some of the need is too painful to see, and the good we can do seems like little more than a drop of water in an ocean of hurt. What difference will it make? Defeated before we ever try, we do nothing. When we draw near to the pain or the need, we also expose ourselves to the possibility that we might well feel some of it within ourselves. That is, in fact, inevitable. It is difficult, too, I believe, because it awakens us to the realization of our own vulnerability. Bad things can and do happen to any of us, even the best of us and the most prepared of us. And, to be completely honest, some of what Jesus calls us to do is, well, *distasteful*. Still, though, Jesus calls us out of our comfort zones and our safety to open our hearts, our arms, ourselves, and our resources to those in need, whoever they may be.

The question for us as followers of Jesus, regardless of our place in life, is not what can I get, but what can I give; not how might I exploit my place in life for personal gain, but how can I use my place in life to make a difference in the lives of others; not what do I deserve, but what can I give in the name of Jesus for the welfare of others?

Competition or Cooperation?
Mark 9:38-41

John said to him, 'Teacher, we saw someone casting out demons in your name, and we tried to stop him, because he was not following us.' But Jesus said, 'Do not stop him; for no one who does a deed of power in my name will be able soon afterwards to speak evil of me. Whoever is not against us is for us. For truly I tell you, whoever gives you a cup of water to drink because you bear the name of Christ will by no means lose the reward.

Worshiping as we do in this magnificent structure, it is sometimes easy to forget that our congregation began not with the construction of this building but some sixty-six years earlier as the First Presbyterian Church of St. Augustine, the second Protestant church to be organized in the previously exclusively Roman Catholic town. In an effort to build some bridges in the fledgling Protestant community, Dr. Mack, the pastor of our congregation, extended an invitation to a new Methodist minister in town, Simon Peter Richardson, to preach at Memorial. Richardson had a reputation of speaking critically of the Calvinists or Presbyterians, but the congregation was nonetheless surprised to hear him condemn our theological tradition from the pulpit of our church declaring: "the whole barbaric system [of Calvinism] ought to have perished in the heathen brain that gave it birth." That took some gall! It wasn't the best of days for building up the unity of the body of Christ in St. Augustine.

In our reading from Mark's gospel today, the disciples of Jesus came to him complaining that they had seen a man "casting out demons in your name," and, they added, "we tried to stop him." Why would they do that? He was doing no harm to anyone. In fact, he was helping. He was bringing healing where there was sickness; wholeness where there was brokenness; freedom where there was bondage, and all in the name of Jesus. Why would they want to stop him? There were, to be sure, more than enough demons lurking about to keep them all busy, but they tried to stop him because, as they explained it, "he was not following us" — not *you* but *us*. The issue would surface again in the early church when others on the outside began to speak and to act in the name of Jesus. What should be done about them? Ignore them? Compete with them? Or denounce them and try to stop them?

There are times and circumstances when the latter is precisely the course the church is called to take. When lies are paraded as truth, when the Christian Gospel is used to legitimize and to forward a particular political or social point of view clearly in conflict with the word of the Gospel, the church is bound to speak up and to challenge the wrong. That was the case for some of the Reformed and Lutheran churches of Germany during the rise of National Socialism prior to the Second World War. At the time there were German Christians who took the union of Christianity, nationalism, and militarism for granted and equated patriotic sentiments with religious truths. Those who had assumed control of the church promoted the concept of a racially pure nation and the iron-fisted rule of Adolph Hitler as God's will for the people of Germany. The Declaration of Barmen, adopted in 1934 by a group of dissidents, challenged that national idolatry and declared the Lordship of Jesus Christ in every aspect of human life, asserting," As the church of pardoned sinners, it has to testify in the midst of a sinful world, with its faith as with its obedience, with its message as with its order, that it is solely [Christ's] property and that it lives and wants to live solely from his comfort and from his direction in the expectation of his appearance." Those who signed this declaration challenged their fellow Christians: "If you find that we are speaking contrary to Scripture, then do not listen to us! But if you find that we are taking our stand upon Scripture, then let no fear or temptation keep you from treading with us the path of faith and obedience to the Word of God." There are times when the church must challenge both those within its ranks and beyond who speak and act in the name of Jesus but whose words and deeds contradict the message of Jesus.

That, however, was not the case with this man. He had stood with the crowd and had heard Jesus teach. He had watched as Jesus healed the sick, liberated the bound, and multiplied loaves and fishes to feed the hungry. Perhaps he himself had felt the touch of Jesus' healing power and had feasted upon the bread blessed by him. Whatever the case, he had watched those who followed Jesus, and now he was seeking to do the work that they did—and was apparently succeeding. So why should they object? Why should they want to stop him? Why do we, if one is really doing the work of Jesus? Jealousy or pride or fear might play a part for us—the fear that they might succeed where we have only modestly succeeded or even failed, or the fear that they might just end up changing us. Different, you see, can be threatening, because it makes us re-examine who we are, what we believe, and why we do the things we do. Poor, indeed, is the Christian who never changes her mind about anything, for she has shut herself off from the witness of scripture and the work of God's Spirit in her life. Numerous have been the times when I have had my own opinions and convictions challenged and changed by the circumstances in my life, a new awareness of the teaching of the Bible, and the work of the Holy Spirit. And, let me tell you, that can be painful. Our resistance, though, like that of John and his fellow disciples, may actually be something far more heinous than jealousy, pride, or fear. More often than not, I think, it is about power—getting it and keeping it.

Whenever people are deeply committed to something, whenever people have invested themselves in something, they will inevitably disagree. In the world those disagreements are resolved by squaring off and slugging it out. The competition is eliminated or at least neutralized, and the one with the power wins the day. In the church of Jesus, it ought not to be so, but too often is. "If I were in control or my group were in control, then we would set things right! Why can't others see things as clearly as we? If these other people, whoever they may be, would just read what Jesus had to say about healing the sick, or feeding the poor, or working for peace, or converting the nations, or keeping the commandments, or whatever it is that we are convinced is the most important aspect of Jesus' work, then surely they would agree with us. How can they be so blind? How can they be so ignorant?" I remember, many years ago now, hearing a pastor, a leader in the church whom I had known all of my life and who I deeply respected, begin his report to Presbytery on the latest General Assembly meeting of what was then the Presbyterian Church in the United States by saying, "We come back to you bloodied, but not beaten." And I recall thinking in my youthful naiveté: "I didn't know we were at war with one another."

So, what do we do with these others, especially when we might feel threatened by them? Compete with them? Denounce them? Capitulate to them? Must we really be against one another? What if, instead of squaring off and slugging it out, we sat down and listened to one another, prayed with and for one another, broke the bread and shared the cup of the Lord's Supper with one another, worshiped beside one another as the brothers and sisters in Jesus Christ that we are? What if we really did acknowledge the fact that in Christ, we are one?

"Do not stop him," said Jesus, "for whoever is not against us is for us." The words are gracious, generous, and express a trust not only in the motives of this unnamed preacher, but, more importantly, in the faithfulness of the heavenly Father to protect and to bring to fulfillment the work of redemption and reconciliation given into his care and to those who follow him. In the meantime, said Jesus, be faithful to your calling, do what you have been called to do, and "be at peace with one another." There is, after all, enough discord in the world and plenty of work to be done.

Forgiveness Is Never Cheap
Luke 7:36-8:3

One of the Pharisees asked Jesus to eat with him, and he went into the Pharisee's house and took his place at the table. And a woman in the city, who was a sinner, having learned that he was eating in the Pharisee's house, brought an alabaster jar of ointment. She stood behind him at his feet, weeping, and began to bathe his feet with her tears and to dry them with her hair. Then she continued kissing his feet and anointing them with the ointment. Now when the Pharisee who had invited him saw it, he said to himself, 'If this man were a prophet, he would have known who and what kind of woman this is who is touching him—that she is a sinner.' Jesus spoke up and said to him, 'Simon, I have something to say to you.' 'Teacher,' he replied, 'speak.' 'A certain creditor had two debtors; one owed five hundred denarii, and the other fifty. When they could not pay, he cancelled the debts for both of them. Now which of them will love him more?' Simon answered, 'I suppose the one for whom he cancelled the greater debt.' And Jesus said to him, 'You have judged rightly.' Then turning towards the woman, he said to Simon, 'Do you see this woman? I entered your house; you gave me no water for my feet, but she has bathed my feet with her tears and dried them with her hair. You gave me no kiss, but from the time I came in she has not stopped kissing my feet. You did not anoint my head with oil, but she has anointed my feet with ointment. Therefore, I tell you, her sins, which were many, have been forgiven; hence she has shown great love. But the one to whom little is forgiven, loves little.' Then he said to her, 'Your sins are forgiven.' But those who were at the table with him began to say among themselves, 'Who is this who even forgives sins?' And he said to the woman, 'Your faith has saved you; go in peace.'

My sister tells the story of how, many years ago now, she arrived late for a party. She didn't recognize anyone right off, but that was ok. It was a large party and she would not have known everyone there. So, she went ahead, had a drink, and entered into the fun. It was only later, after a couple more drinks and having become a part of one group of partiers, that she realized she was at the wrong party. She started to leave, but her new-found friends implored her to stay, and she did. That party, she said, was a lot more fun than the one she was invited to.

My sister attended a party by mistake, but she was welcomed there. The party we read about in our Gospel lesson this morning was quite different. The woman in that story was neither invited nor wanted. Luke leaves little room for doubt regarding this woman's way of life. She wasn't one who, in the midst of an otherwise morally upright life, had managed to stumble in some indiscretion. She made her living, she survived, by trading with the only asset she possessed—her body. Never mind the personal, social, and economic powers that may have pushed her into this life; that's where she was and what she did. In many respects, she was a non-entity—quite simply, disposable. If she turned up dead in some dark alley, no one would have missed her, no one would have mourned her dying, no one would have cared, for there was no one left to care.

Kneeling at Jesus' feet, she began to weep, perhaps softly at first, her tears streaming from her face to his feet. With no towel or cloth at hand, she dried the Lord's feet with her flowing hair, kissed them, and then anointed them with the oil she had brought with her. Were they tears of sadness, of regret, of shame? I expect so, but they were also tears of incredible joy and gratitude. She had experienced something with Jesus she had never experienced with any other man. Unlike the others, he neither wanted anything from her nor did he stand in scornful judgment of her. In his eyes, she knew, she was not merely an object to be used and then discarded, but a person of value in her own right, a person to be known and loved for who she was.

Simon was scandalized not only that this happened at his dinner party, but that Jesus did nothing to stop her. "If this man were a prophet," he thought to himself, "he would have known who and what kind of woman this is who is touching him, that she is a sinner, and he would do something to make her stop this obscene display." Of course, Jesus knew precisely what kind of woman she was, and knowing, too, what his host was thinking, Jesus told this short story. "A certain creditor had two debtors; one owed him 500 hundred denarii, the other fifty. When they could not pay, he cancelled the debts of both of them." It is interesting to note that here Jesus likens the forgiveness of sins to the forgiveness of a debt. The entire lives and futures of the Galilean peasants who first heard this teaching were bound up in the debt they owed to landowners or shopkeepers. Like sharecroppers, they lived from one crop to the next, buying seed and fertilizer on credit against the anticipated crop. One disaster, one failed crop, could dig a financial hole from which there was little or no opportunity for escape. Their lives and futures were no longer their own; they belonged to someone else. To be freed from that debt would mean an entirely new life.

At the conclusion of the story, Jesus asked his host which of the two debtors would feel the greatest love for the one who had forgiven their debt. "I suppose the one for whom he cancelled the greater debt," Simon answered. He was correct, of course, but he missed the point. While the woman's debt, at least from the perspective of her culture, was the greater of the two, Simon was like her, a debtor, too. As different as were their worlds, Simon and this unnamed woman held one thing in common—both of them were sinners, both of them needed what Jesus had to give: forgiveness, a new beginning, a new life. The distinction was that she recognized her need, while Simon was blind to his. Everything in this Pharisee's life focused on doing the right thing, on keeping the minutest details of the Law and thus making himself acceptable to God. To have admitted to being a sinner would have brought down his whole house of cards. You see, it was his very goodness—and Simon was a good man—that blinded him to his pride and his hypocrisy, to his need for God's forgiving grace.

We, like Simon, are people who take our religious profession seriously, who seek to obey the law, to love God and our neighbor, and to live morally upright lives. The irony is that sometimes for us, like Simon, it is this very goodness for which we have striven that presents the greatest obstacle to our spiritual growth. Jesus was crucified not because he called into question the worst that is within us, but because he dared to challenge the adequacy of our best, our hard-earned best, to gain for us that for which we most deeply and earnestly yearn—life, full and eternal life.

Jesus explained to his host, "I entered your house; you gave me no water for my feet, but she has bathed my feet with her tears and dried them with her hair. You gave me no kiss, but from the time I came in she has not stopped kissing my feet. You did not anoint my head with oil, but she has anointed my feet with ointment." She welcomed Jesus; Simon did not. "Your faith has saved you," Jesus said to this woman—your *faith*, not your good works, not your moral purity or hard-earned goodness—but your faith. Our deliverance from brokenness to wholeness, from slavery to freedom, from death to life is through the simple act of trusting, trusting Jesus to do for us what we cannot do for ourselves. What makes this trust possible, I think, is the reception Jesus gives us when we turn to him empty-handed and open-hearted: "Come unto me, all you who labor and are heavily burdened and I will give you rest," he promises—rest from your weariness, from the burdens that weigh you down, from the fears that wake you in the night, from the worries that eat away at you, from the guilt that plagues you. He doesn't admonish: "Come back when you have it all together or when you can prove yourself worthy of my love," but "Come to me now with all your imperfections, all your burdens, all your failures, your hard earned best, just as you are, and I will give you rest. I will make you whole.

The church is composed, I think, of both Pharisees and "sinners." In truth, there is a little of each in all of us. Like the woman who crashed the dinner party at Simon's house we, too, know what it is to be bound and to yearn for freedom. Like Simon, we, too, have suffered from spiritual and moral blind spots that have kept us from seeing the wrong in our own lives while we have been hasty and harsh in our judgments of others for the wrongs, we have seen in theirs. "In two thousand years of practice we haven't gotten any better," writes Eugene Peterson. "You would think that we would have, but we haven't. Every time we open up a church door and take a careful, scrutinizing look inside we find them there again—sinners. [And] also Christ, Christ in the preaching, Christ in the sacraments, but inconveniently and embarrassingly mixed up into this congregation of sinners."[15] Jesus keeps the strangest company, don't you think?

---

[15] Eugene Peterson, *Under the Unpredictable Plant*, (William B. Eerdman's Publishing Company, Grand Rapids, 1994), 24,

"Go in peace," were the last words Jesus spoke to this grateful woman. But where was she to go? If this were a "Christian romance novel," she would have been swept away by some noble man who loved her despite her ignoble past, and they would live happily ever after. But this isn't fiction; this was real life. The only place where she was truly welcomed was on the street, among her own, back in the old life. What she needed was a new community, a community of grace and forgiveness, a community of forgiven and forgiving sinners, a community still in the process of being transformed by the work of the Holy Spirit and the love and fellowship of God's people. What she needed was the church, and not just any church, but a church like this one that says: "You are welcome here, just as you are, with all of your fears and foibles, your successes and failures, your struggles and disappointments. You are welcome here. Come, take your place here with us at Christ's table and join us in the journey to wholeness through the forgiving and life-renewing grace of God in Jesus Christ."

Facing Formidable Foes
Mark 4:35-41

On that day, when evening had come, he said to them, 'Let us go across to the other side.' And leaving the crowd behind, they took him with them in the boat, just as he was. Other boats were with him. A great gale arose, and the waves beat into the boat, so that the boat was already being swamped. But he was in the stern, asleep on the cushion; and they woke him up and said to him, 'Teacher, do you not care that we are perishing?' He woke up and rebuked the wind, and said to the sea, 'Peace! Be still!' Then the wind ceased, and there was a dead calm. He said to them, 'Why are you afraid? Have you still no faith?' And they were filled with great awe and said to one another, 'Who then is this, that even the wind and the sea obey him?'

Shortly after we moved to St. Augustine, good, new friends invited Mary and me to join them and another couple on their boat for a little sail around the harbor. It was a beautiful day—clear skies, a gentle breeze, and not terribly hot. We stepped aboard filled with anticipation of a wonderful time, but no less than thirty seconds after accepting the invitation to see the living quarters below deck, I knew I had made a mistake, a big mistake – and we had yet to leave the dock! While all the others aboard enjoyed the view, the warm sun, and delicious food and libations, I sported an unenviable shade of green as I sipped cautiously on a warm Ginger Ale.

Jesus and the twelve, exhausted by a day of teaching, attentive listening, and interaction with yet another crowd eager to hear the good news, boarded a boat and settled down to enjoy a restful crossing of the lake. After the noise and push of the day, the quiet of a nighttime sail offered the chance for a bit of solitude, for some sleep, for renewal. But that restful crossing soon turned into a harrowing struggle for their very lives as the wind unexpectedly picked up and soon turned into a howling storm. The waves beat against the boat, the wind tore at her sails, and the small vessel was tossed about like a toy in a child's hand.

As the disciples feared for their lives, clinging desperately to the boat that pitched and rolled in the water, Jesus was "dead to the world," asleep on a cushion in the stern of the craft—oblivious to the danger that threatened him and them, and deaf to the fearful cries of his friends. Shaking him awake, they asked, "Teacher, do you not care that we are perishing?" "Can't you see what is happening here? Wake up! Do you not care?" You wonder sometimes, you really do. You struggle; you fight; you give the best that you have to give; you plead, and you pray and none of it seems to make a bit of difference. "Lord, can't you see what is happening here? Why don't you do something?" Is it that he is preoccupied with someone or something more important? Is he simply oblivious? Or is it that he really doesn't care if you sink or swim, live or die? You wonder sometimes. You do.

Some things in life come upon us like an unexpected storm in the midst of an otherwise peaceful sail. You're just floating along, minding your own business, doing whatever it is that you are supposed to be doing and then— "bam"— out of nowhere it hits you. There are other things that are not thrust upon us, but which we ourselves choose to face— things which, perhaps, we have managed rather successfully to avoid or excuse or simply ignore for the longest of times, or things which for whatever reason we feel called, if not compelled, to confront—and in choosing to face them we find ourselves staring up at Goliath-sized challenges. In our Old Testament lesson the Philistine giant taunted the defenders of Israel: "Choose a man for yourselves and let him come down to me. If he is able to fight with me and kill me, then we will be your servants; but if I prevail against him and kill him, then you shall be our servants." There was not a man among them who was willing to stand up to the challenge until David, still little more than a boy, stepped forward. It was folly, they knew, pure folly, but King Saul nonetheless dressed the boy in his own armor and put his sword into his hand. (Even folly ought to be properly equipped.) Who knew? Maybe by some stroke of luck he might actually succeed. The youth, though, found the heavy and ill-fitting armor more a hindrance than a help. Casting it aside he went forth to face the foe as he would a bear or lion threatening his father's flock—with a few stones in his pouch and a sling in his hand.

Some might say, and not unreasonably at all, that it was a combination of desperation and naiveté that sent David forth to face Goliath—Saul's desperation and David's naiveté—but David had something else, something which Saul had lost and which apparently was not yet fully developed in the frightened disciples of Jesus—faith, that is trust in God's unfailing care and purpose. "This very day the Lord will deliver you into my hand," cried the youth to the giant, "so that all the earth may know that there is a God in Israel and that all this assembly may know that the Lord does not save by sword and spear; for the battle is the Lord's and he will give you into my hand." That is not to say that the Lord's choice of armament is five stones and a sling, as opposed to sword and spear, but that the power and purpose of God transcend all human strength and power.

It is only natural for us to find a sense of security in the defenses that we manage to erect for ourselves: our accumulated assets in the face of financial challenge; our knowledge in the face of new and potentially frightening things; our accessibility to the best medical care in the face of life-threatening illness, and the power of superior armaments, personnel and defense systems in the face of threats posed by other nations and groups. But all of these have their limits, and deep down inside us somewhere is the realization that despite our best preparations, ultimately we cannot safeguard ourselves and those we love from all danger. No doubt the disciples believed the boat that carried them and Jesus was seaworthy. No doubt they had every confidence in their navigational and sailing skills;

after all, they were professionals. But the storm in which they found themselves by no fault of their own—like the giant standing before young David—far exceeded the strength and knowledge they themselves had to bring. The difference is that while David recognized that his help was from the Lord and faced the foe with confidence born of that assurance, the disciples faltered in their faith. "Why are you afraid?" asked Jesus. "Have you still no faith?' That is, after all you have seen and heard and experienced with me, do you still not trust me to care for you?

There are times when the Lord speaks, "Peace. Be still!" and the raging of the storm subsides, the danger passes. But there are also times when the word is spoken, and the storm continues to rage. What changes is not the tumult around us, but the terror within us. Anyone who has struggled with an addiction can tell you that. They do not speak of themselves as having recovered, but only as *recovering*. The threat to their health and happiness, the enemy, never goes away. What changes is something inside. With the help of a higher power the fear is faced, a choice is made, and a new life is begun. That higher power, we know, is God's grace and love poured out upon us in Jesus Christ. The storm about us may continue unabated, but the terror gives way to a calm, to a peace that passes all understanding.

A hymn whose words I have reflected on in times of struggle assures us:

I look to Thee in every need, and never look in vain;

I feel Thy strong and tender love, and all is well again;
The thought of Thee is mightier far
than sin and want and sorrow are.
Discouraged in the work of life, disheartened by its load;
Shamed by its failures or its fears, I sink beside the road;
But let me only think of Thee
and then new heart springs up in me.

In those times when you find yourself confronting challenges and situations, even potentially life-changing or life-threatening circumstances either from forces beyond your control, like the disciples, or through your own conscious choice, like David, remember you are not alone. Jesus is in the boat with you, Jesus is beside you, and Jesus will guide you through the storm to the calm waters beyond the wind and the waves.

Where Are You God?
Exodus 17:1-7

From the wilderness of Sin the whole congregation of the Israelites journeyed by stages, as the Lord commanded. They camped at Rephidim, but there was no water for the people to drink. The people quarreled with Moses, and said, 'Give us water to drink.' Moses said to them, 'Why do you quarrel with me? Why do you test the Lord?' But the people thirsted there for water; and the people complained against Moses and said, 'Why did you bring us out of Egypt, to kill us and our children and livestock with thirst?' So Moses cried out to the Lord, 'What shall I do with this people? They are almost ready to stone me.' The Lord said to Moses, 'Go on ahead of the people, and take some of the elders of Israel with you; take in your hand the staff with which you struck the Nile and go. I will be standing there in front of you on the rock at Horeb. Strike the rock, and water will come out of it, so that the people may drink.' Moses did so, in the sight of the elders of Israel. He called the place Massah and Meribah, because the Israelites quarreled and tested the Lord, saying, 'Is the Lord among us or not?'

Things happen, bad things, unfortunate things, unjust things, unthinkable things happen, and what makes them so very hard to understand sometimes is when they happen for no apparent reason, striking out of the blue. Just as mystifying, perhaps even more so, is when bad things happen, not as a result of some unknown evil power or as the result of your own poor choices, but as a result of your having done the right thing. "No good deed goes unpunished," goes the saying, and some of us, I imagine, can testify to that.

When the Hebrew slaves escaped their bondage in Egypt, I don't imagine that any of them believed the way before them was going to be particularly easy, but neither were there any misgivings about a run for freedom being the right thing to do. They were accustomed to hardship and struggle. The life of slavery is anything but pleasant, but what they encountered in the fresh air of freedom was far more difficult than any of them had anticipated. If they had known ahead of time what lay before them, I wonder how many really would have left the old life behind. We're not talking about lacking luxuries, but rather the basic necessities of life. No sooner had they crossed the border than Pharaoh changed his mind about allowing them to go peacefully, and sent his troops in hot pursuit, and they stared death in the face. Then it was hunger, and in our reading today, thirst. Through parched lips and dry throats, they demanded of their leader Moses: "Give us water to drink." And then they accused: "Why did you bring us out of Egypt; to kill us and our children and our livestock with thirst?"

I suppose you could characterize their lament as rather ungrateful. Where was their faith? God had already done so much for them—broken the shackles that bound them, parted the waters of the sea to rescue them, provided quail in the evening and manna in the morning to satisfy their hunger. Why couldn't they trust God to provide once more? When you know how the story turns out, it is easy to think that way, but in the midst of it, well, that's a different matter. You see, the issue for the Israelites in the wilderness was far more profound than water or food or hostile enemies. At the heart of their complaint was the question: "Is the Lord among us or not?" Has God brought us out here simply to abandon us? Is this our reward for obedience to God's command? Where are God's promises now? Where is God now? Does God even care?

The people of Israel did not deny the reality of God or the power of God. What they questioned was the goodness of God. If God is indeed love, if it is really true that God is sovereign, that God has the whole world in his hands, if God is really God, how can these things happen? How can God allow this to happen, or, worse yet, how could God intend for such a thing to happen? A pastor I knew who had experienced more than his own share of tragedy and loss in life, once preached a sermon with his back to the congregation, facing a large wooden cross that graced the sanctuary. Rather than proclaiming God's word to the people that day, he took the opportunity to face God with the gathered complaints of the people of God. It was, to be sure, an unusual homiletical approach and one not appreciated by everyone in church that Sunday, but what he did was not all unlike what the psalmist did when he lamented before the Almighty: "Rouse yourself! Why do you sleep, O Lord? Awake, do not cast us off forever! Why do you hide your face? Why do you forget our affliction and oppression? For we sink down to the dust; our bodies cling to the ground. Rise up, come to our help. Redeem us for the sake of your steadfast love." (Psa. 44:22-23)

Is the Lord among us or not? You wonder sometimes, you really do. You pray for healing, but the struggle continues until death alone brings the longed-for end to pain and suffering. You pray for guidance, but rather than a clear-cut path to follow, you are given a variety of options from which to choose—none of them what you were expecting. You pray for release from a burden, but it just won't go away. You pray for an answer, but one never comes. You plead for understanding, but still it eludes you. God disappoints us when he doesn't respond in the way that it seems to us God ought to respond. We look for God in the burning bush that is not consumed; in the separation of the waters providing a path of deliverance from danger; in the miracle of manna from heaven, or in the water gushing from the rock, but God's answers to our pleas are not always constructed out of the stuff of our expectations, and when he does not answer as we expect we often assume that he must be otherwise occupied, asleep, or worse yet unconcerned with our plight. We look for God in the grand and glorious, and while we have seen the glory and grandeur of what he has done and is capable of doing, much of God's work is unseen and unrecognized until it breaks forth in our lives—in the daily strength and courage it takes to live with a debilitating illness; in the quiet peace that descends in the wake of the death of one you loved more than life; in the inexplicable hope that rises within you when every reason for hope has died; in the fortitude with which you are able to face up to unwanted changes in your life, in light to find your way through the darkness. Sometimes, too, it is in the hand of a friend, your spouse, a brother or sister in faith, or maybe even a complete stranger who reaches out a hand and walks beside you. St. Paul tells us that he prayed again and again that God might cure him of a physical malady that from his perspective made his work for Christ less effective than it might be if he were healed. The answer that ultimately came was: "My grace is sufficient for you, for my strength is made perfect in weakness." It was not what he expected, not what he wanted, but all that he needed.

"God moves in a mysterious way his wonders to perform," the hymn tells us, and perhaps most mysterious of all, at least from the human perspective, is God's most intimate movement among us. "Christ Jesus, though he was in the form of God, did not count equality with God as something to be exploited," writes St. Paul, "but emptied himself, taking the form of a slave, being born in human likeness. And being found in human form, he humbled himself and became obedient unto the point of death—even death on a cross." How un-god-like is that? But if God so deigned to come among us, to walk beside us and with us, even to suffer and die for us, how much more can we trust that in whatever quandary we may find ourselves today, whatever loss we must endure, whatever question we must live with, whatever challenge we must face, surely still he walks beside us and with us and will give us what we need to endure and in enduring to overcome.

Things happen, hard and inexplicable things. Sometimes you can make sense of them; most of the time you cannot. But there is one thing of which we can always be sure: the God who has delivered us from our bondage, redeeming us in Jesus Christ, continues with us in the journey and will see us all the way to the end. Lament, if you must. Complain to God. There is absolutely nothing wrong in that. The psalms are rich with the sound of lament, but, like the psalmists, we can also conclude our laments with a word of thanks for the deliverance—whatever form it may take—that we know God in his goodness will provide. Things happen, things that make no sense at all, but this we know and of this we can be certain: the God who called us forth walks with us and will give us what we need.

Seeing Clearly
John 9:1-33

As he walked along, he saw a man blind from birth. His disciples asked him, 'Rabbi, who sinned, this man or his parents, that he was born blind?' Jesus answered, 'Neither this man nor his parents sinned; he was born blind so that God's works might be revealed in him. We must work the works of him who sent me while it is day; night is coming when no one can work. As long as I am in the world, I am the light of the world.' When he had said this, he spat on the ground and made mud with the saliva and spread the mud on the man's eyes, saying to him, 'Go, wash in the pool of Siloam' (which means Sent). Then he went and washed and came back able to see. The neighbors and those who had seen him before as a beggar began to ask, 'Is this not the man who used to sit and beg?' Some were saying, 'It is he.' Others were saying, 'No, but it is someone like him.' He kept saying, 'I am the man.' But they kept asking him, 'Then how were your eyes opened?' He answered, 'The man called Jesus made mud, spread it on my eyes, and said to me, "Go to Siloam and wash." Then I went and washed and received my sight.' They said to him, 'Where is he?' He said, 'I do not know.'

They brought to the Pharisees the man who had formerly been blind. Now it was a sabbath day when Jesus made the mud and opened his eyes. Then the Pharisees also began to ask him how he had received his sight. He said to them, 'He put mud on my eyes. Then I washed, and now I see.' Some of the Pharisees said, 'This man is not from God, for he does not observe the sabbath.' But others said, 'How can a man who is a sinner perform such signs?' And they were divided. So they said again to the blind man, 'What do you say about him? It was your eyes he opened.' He said, 'He is a prophet.'

The Jews did not believe that he had been blind and had received his sight until they called the parents of the man who had received his sight and asked them, 'Is this your son, who you say was born blind? How then does he now see?' His parents answered, 'We know that this is our son, and that he was born blind; but we do not know how it is that now he sees, nor do we know who opened his eyes. Ask him; he is of age. He will speak for himself.' His parents said this because they were afraid of the Jews; for the Jews had already agreed that anyone who confessed Jesus to be the Messiah would be put out of the synagogue. Therefore, his parents said, 'He is of age; ask him.'

So for the second time they called the man who had been blind, and they said to him, 'Give glory to God! We know that this man is a sinner.' He answered, 'I do not know whether he is a sinner. One thing I do know, that though I was blind, now I see.' They said to him, 'What did he do to you? How did he open your eyes?' He answered them, 'I have told you already, and you would not listen. Why do you want to hear it again? Do you also want to become his disciples?' Then they reviled him, saying, 'You are his disciple, but we are disciples of Moses. We know that God has spoken to Moses, but as for this man, we do not know where he comes from.' The man answered, 'Here is an astonishing thing! You do not know where he comes from, and yet he opened my eyes. We know that God does not listen to sinners, but he does listen to one who worships him and obeys his will. Never since the world began has it been heard that anyone opened the eyes of a person born blind. If this man were not from God, he could do nothing.' 34They answered him, 'You were born entirely in sins, and are you trying to teach us?' And they drove him out.

Most days, with the exception of my day off, I routinely wear a black clerical shirt, clerical collar, and gray slacks—sometimes khaki or blue, but mostly gray. Aside from professional considerations there is a rather pragmatic one for my choice of clothing. It isn't that I can't tell my colors—most preschoolers can do that. It's that I do not see all of them clearly. Green, brown, pink, gray, and sometimes red are the particularly annoying ones, as they often masquerade as something else. It is not a colorless world I see, only a differently-colored one.

There are times for all of us when we see things clearly. The colors in our world complement one another, and everything is as it should be. But there are also times when things are shaded or completely unseen: when we are blind to the true motives of another; blind to what our child is doing right under your nose; blind to the pain in our spouse's eyes; blind to our own self-destructive behavior, blind to the faults within ourselves and within others. Often, too, we are blind to what is wrong in the world and to what God calls us to do about it, not out of any meanness of spirit or conscious choice to go along with the way of evil, but out of ignorance, naiveté, or simply uncritical conformity to the world around us. "It's just the way things are," we say, and we go along.

I remember from my childhood the thrill of riding the city bus home from downtown with a friend. It was a great adventure for both of us. I remember, too, thinking how much fun it would be to sit on the bench that stretched across the back of the bus. It seemed to sway and bounce with such energy. So, friend and I decided to sit in the back of the bus—until, that is, the driver stopped the bus, walked to the back, and, peering down at us, sternly warned us to move to the front where little white boys belonged or to get the [expletive deleted] off his bus. No one had ever told us that *we* weren't supposed to sit there, that somehow it was wrong by prevailing cultural standards. The truth is that we were wrong about a lot of things in those days. We were wrong about racial segregation, wrong in denying equal rights to all persons, wrong about the causes of mental illness, wrong about alcoholism and other addictive behaviors, wrong about a lot of things. For that matter, we still are. The greater sin, though, is the refusal to entertain the possibility that we might indeed *be* wrong. That's the problem Jesus had with the Pharisees.

They were, for the most part, people who meant well, who took their religious faith and commitment seriously, and who strove with all their might to be the kind of people they thought God wanted them to be, which in their case meant meticulously keeping the rules. They were the religious elite, the most well-informed, theologically educated, biblically literate people of their day, yet they were also self-righteously narrow-minded and judgmental. Those who ostensibly knew God best did not recognize his truth when it stared them in the face. The offense they took at Jesus on the occasion recorded in our Gospel lesson for today was not so much that he broke the law by making mud with his spittle and spreading it on the blind man's eyes on the Sabbath, but that he had the audacity, the sheer audacity, to challenge them, their perspectives, their opinions, and their deeply-held religious and social convictions. In fact, said Jesus, they were as good as blind to the things that matter most—to truth, to love, to God and God's will. Ironic, isn't it, that those who thought they saw most clearly of all couldn't see a thing? Jesus reserved his harshest judgment not for those who stumbled or even jumped headlong into some pit of moral failure, but for those who, believing they alone knew the truth, judged and condemned all who failed to conform to their perception of the truth.

When you trust him, when you allow him into your life, Jesus will open your eyes to an entirely different perception of reality, indeed an altogether new reality which cannot be known apart from him. It is shaped not by human customs and traditions, but by the will of God. It is an upside-down sort of world in comparison with the world of ordinary human affairs. It is a world in which being the servant is more highly valued than being the one who can command service; in which generosity is the true measure of wealth; in which forgiveness is far more highly valued than the capacity to settle the score . . . you get the idea. St. Paul exhorts us: "Do not be conformed to this world, but be transformed by the renewing of your minds, so that you may discern what is the will of God—what is good and acceptable and perfect." (Romans 12:1-2) That is the life to which we are called as followers of Jesus; a life in which the fundamental question that shapes all of our choices is, "What would Jesus have me do in this time and in this particular circumstance?" There are times, to be sure, when we know beyond a shadow of a doubt what that is. After all, Jesus said, "I am the Way, the Truth, and the Life." It should be cut and dried, black and white, but it isn't always, is it? There are times when we are torn by uncertainty, by question, by doubt. A shade of gray is the best we can do. These are the times of significant moral and ethical struggle in our lives. Very often it is easier not to enter into them, but to fall back on time-worn practices and prejudices rather than re-evaluating thoughts and customs that are second nature to us. There are times when we find ourselves embracing a kind of moral relativism that reduces the truth to a matter of personal preference, so that truth is always relative—relative to what I think is true, what serves my purposes, what suits my passions at the moment—but that, too, avoids the question of what is right, what really is true, what God intends.

This does not mean that we are to be forever equivocating. Martin Luther declared, "Here I stand. I can do no other. God help me." Had he not, the sixteenth century Reformation of the Church might well be little more than a footnote on the page. There are times when we must stand up and declare what we believe God is calling us to do and then *do* it. We do that, though, recognizing that we are limited by time and space and knowledge, and that even our most noble convictions and actions are distorted by self-interest and sin. Our perception of truth, our understanding of God's gracious will and purpose, is always provisional.

We come to truth, our eyes are opened, not through any superior insight of our own, but only by grace. As John Newton's much-beloved hymn reminds us: "Amazing grace, how sweet the sound, that saved a wretch like me. I once was lost, but now am found; was blind, but now I see." It is Jesus who opens our eyes to the truth, God's truth, and that truth comes to us not in one all-encompassing epiphany, but over a lifetime as we continue our walk with Jesus and grow more and more into his likeness.

The Road to Emmaus
Luke 24:13-35

Now on that same day two of them were going to a village called Emmaus, about seven miles from Jerusalem, and talking with each other about all these things that had happened. While they were talking and discussing, Jesus himself came near and went with them, but their eyes were kept from recognizing him. And he said to them, 'What are you discussing with each other while you walk along?' They stood still, looking sad. Then one of them, whose name was Cleopas, answered him, 'Are you the only stranger in Jerusalem who does not know the things that have taken place there in these days?' He asked them, 'What things?' They replied, 'The things about Jesus of Nazareth, who was a prophet mighty in deed and word before God and all the people, and how our chief priests and leaders handed him over to be condemned to death and crucified him. But we had hoped that he was the one to redeem Israel. Yes, and besides all this, it is now the third day since these things took place. Moreover, some women of our group astounded us. They were at the tomb early this morning, and when they did not find his body there, they came back and told us that they had indeed seen a vision of angels who said that he was alive. Some of those who were with us went to the tomb and found it just as the women had said; but they did not see him.' Then he said to them, 'Oh, how foolish you are, and how slow of heart to believe all that the prophets have declared! Was it not necessary that the Messiah should suffer these things and then enter into his glory?' Then beginning with Moses and all the prophets, he interpreted to them the things about himself in all the scriptures.

As they came near the village to which they were going, he walked ahead as if he were going on. But they urged him strongly, saying, 'Stay with us, because it is almost evening and the day is now nearly over.' So he went in to stay with them. When he was at the table with them, he took bread, blessed and broke it, and gave it to them. Then their eyes were opened, and they recognized him; and he vanished from their sight. They said to each other, 'Were not our hearts burning within us while he was talking to us on the road, while he was opening the scriptures to us?' That same hour they got up and returned to Jerusalem; and they found the eleven and their companions gathered together. They were saying, 'The Lord has risen indeed, and he has appeared to Simon!' Then they told what had happened on the road, and how he had been made known to them in the breaking of the bread.

There is no way to know why they were going to Emmaus. Maybe it was home for them; maybe they had business there now that the Sabbath was over; or maybe it was just a place to go—a place to get away from it all, to forget if only a little while the disappointment, the grief, the sadness that hovered over them. You don't really expect to find any answers in Emmaus, just a little peace, a little quiet. Cleopas and his companion had been followers of Jesus. They had been in Jerusalem, had seen or at least heard about his death on the cross. They had placed their hopes in him, but all that had come crashing down around them, and now they just needed to get away from it all.

Life is like that sometimes, isn't it? A relationship you thought was going somewhere abruptly ends; a loved one dies; your family falls apart; your career plateaus; a friend betrays you; your faith crumbles; boredom envelops you; or maybe you finally arrive at what had been your life's goal, only to discover that the prize in your hand is not at all what you expected it to be, and you realize that in spite of your best efforts you are still more lost than found, more empty than full. Anger, disappointment, grief, sadness descends like an oppressive fog from which there seems no escape. You just have to get away, away from it all, and off you go to Emmaus. "Emmaus" may be a stool at a local tavern, a workout at the gym, a jog along the beach, a hike in the wilderness, time working in your garden, the feel of your fingers moving across the piano keyboard, making music with your friends, sitting in a quiet sanctuary, or gathering here with others in praise, thanksgiving, and intercession before the living God.

The truth is that we don't really forget anything in Emmaus. Its advantage is that it provides us with the space we need to process things, to see things from a different perspective. Sometimes we get so caught up in the immediacy of things that we cannot see the whole of it. That, I think, was what Cleopas and his companion were doing as they walked along the road. There were, I imagine, long stretches of silence when each of them was absorbed in his own thinking, but there were also times when they talked about all that had happened in Jerusalem and what that meant for their own lives. A stranger came up alongside them and said, in effect, "Hey guys! What's up?" It was an innocent enough question, but Luke tells us that it stopped them dead in their tracks, and "they stood still, looking sad." Sad not only because of what had happened, but sad because this man had no idea of what had happened. It was the only thing they could think about, but it wasn't even on this stranger's radar screen. Somehow his ignorance made Jesus' death seem even more futile and the loss, their loss, more overwhelming. How could life just go on? Cleopas gathered himself, though, and told the story of the whole weekend, including the account of the empty tomb and the not-yet-believed claim of resurrection. To their surprise, the stranger took what he had been told and, beginning with Moses and the prophets interpreted for them the meaning of Jesus' life and ministry in the context of the promises of God. When they arrived at their destination, though the stranger apparently intended to continue his journey, they prevailed upon him to remain the night with them, in part because it was late and in part because they wanted to hear more from him. It wasn't until they shared the evening meal with him, and he broke, blessed, and gave the bread to them that they recognized him, and he was gone. How could they not have recognized him?

Luke tells us that it was not entirely their own obtuseness that kept them from seeing Jesus for who he was. As they began their journey, the narrative informs us their eyes were "kept" from recognizing Jesus. God does not force new understandings upon us but prepares us to receive the revelations he has in store for us. These two were not yet ready to see Jesus. It was only after they had recounted the story to him, he had put it into the context of the whole of Scripture for them, and he took bread, broke it, and gave it to them that "their eyes were opened, and they recognized him." Fred Craddock writes: "There are three times in which we know an event: in rehearsal, at the time of the event, and in remembrance. In rehearsal, understanding is hindered by an inability to believe that the event will really occur or that it will be so important. At the time of the event understanding is hindered by the clutter and confusion of so much so fast. But in remembrance, the non-seriousness of rehearsal and the busyness of the event give way to recognition, realization, and understanding. [Remembrance] is a time of understanding of an important trip, a wedding, a gathering of friends, or a conversation with a stranger turned Christ at table."[16] Remembrance is when it all comes together.

Very often, as with Cleopas and his companion on the road to Emmaus, it is only after the fact that we recognize that Christ has walked beside us—in the voice of a stranger or a friend, in a child's unexpected gift, in an embrace, in the words of a book, the glory of a sunrise or a sunset. But there is one place and time where it is promised, and that is here and now. Here in the gathering, in the prayers and songs, in the reading and preaching of God's word, in the music and

---

[16] Fred Craddock, *Interpretation: Luke,* John Knox Press, 1990, p. 287

the quiet, in the breaking of the bread and the sharing of the cup, Christ himself is present with us and offers himself to us anew as the very bread of life. Some of these holy moments are more momentous than others, but what really makes the difference is the recurring experience. What we discover is that here the "Jerusalems" of our lives are put into perspective, and in time, by the grace of God, are transformed from places of devastating defeat into places of new beginnings and new life in the context of God's eternal purpose.

When we go forth from here into the world, it is with the conviction that no matter how disappointing, painful, and overwhelming the "Jerusalems" of our lives may appear to be, they no longer have the last word over us. In the resurrection of Jesus from death to life, God has triumphed over the power of sin and death. Because Christ lives, we too shall live, and this world of God's making will live anew.

When they left Jerusalem, Cleopas and his friend thought that their world was over. Looking back, they realized that it was only beginning, as was the life of the world.

A Cruel Story
Genesis 21:8-21

The child grew and was weaned; and Abraham made a great feast on the day that Isaac was weaned. But Sarah saw the son of Hagar the Egyptian, whom she had borne to Abraham, playing with her son Isaac. So she said to Abraham, 'Cast out this slave woman with her son; for the son of this slave woman shall not inherit along with my son Isaac.' The matter was very distressing to Abraham on account of his son. But God said to Abraham, 'Do not be distressed because of the boy and because of your slave woman; whatever Sarah says to you, do as she tells you, for it is through Isaac that offspring shall be named after you. As for the son of the slave woman, I will make a nation of him also, because he is your offspring.' So Abraham rose early in the morning, and took bread and a skin of water, and gave it to Hagar, putting it on her shoulder, along with the child, and sent her away. And she departed and wandered about in the wilderness of Beer-Sheba.

When the water in the skin was gone, she cast the child under one of the bushes. Then she went and sat down opposite him a good way off, about the distance of a bowshot; for she said, 'Do not let me look on the death of the child.' And as she sat opposite him, she lifted up her voice and wept. And God heard the voice of the boy; and the angel of God called to Hagar from heaven, and said to her, 'What troubles you, Hagar? Do not be afraid; for God has heard the voice of the boy where he is. Come, lift up the boy and hold him fast with your hand, for I will make a great nation of him.' Then God opened her eyes, and she saw a well of water. She went, and filled the skin with water, and gave the boy a drink.

God was with the boy, and he grew up; he lived in the wilderness and became an expert with the bow. He lived in the wilderness of Paran; and his mother got a wife for him from the land of Egypt.

It is a cruel story—this narrative of Hagar and Ishmael—but the Bible is no stranger to cruelty, for it is the narrative of the interplay between humanity's sin and God's unfolding mercy. When Abraham and Sarah had been summoned from their home and tribe in Haran with the promise of a land of their own, it had also been with the assurance that through them God would bring into being a great nation, through whom his blessing would be bestowed upon all the nations. It was a huge promise that ultimately hinged upon the birth of at least one child. Sarah had been unable to conceive and, as the years passed, her barrenness not only became from the biblical narrative's point of view a threat to the fulfillment of the promise, but more personally an aching, painful void in her life. Every part of her being yearned for the gift of a child. Well past the age of childbearing, Sarah turned to a practice, abhorrent to us, but accepted in her culture. She "gave" her maid Hagar to Abraham to bear a child in her stead. Hagar, an Egyptian slave in the household, had no voice, no vote in the matter. The scheme, however, backfired on Sarah when Hagar, the powerless one, discovered that her ability to conceive and to bear a child gave her at least an emotional power over her mistress, and Sarah resented it to the core. In time, though, God's promise was kept, and Sarah, beyond all odds, conceived and bore a son, Isaac. Her enmity towards Hagar, however, did not go away.

Our text for today picks up the story with a family scene in which Isaac and his older half-brother Ishmael are playing. Abraham looks on with pleasure as his two sons play, but Sarah with resentment and anger. She hated Hagar for her success in bearing a child and she hated Ishmael for his place in his father's affection, but her greatest ire focused on the possibility—in her mind at least—that Ishmael might share in Isaac's inheritance from his father. Though born of a slave he was, after all, Abraham's firstborn. And so, she demanded that Ismael and Hagar be expelled from the family circle which, of course, meant almost certain death. Early the next morning Abraham, acquiescing to his wife's demands, sent Hagar and Ishmael into the wilderness with only some bread and a skin of water to sustain them. If they survived, it would be a miracle. One part of us wants to cry out in objection to this injustice: "No! No! This is wrong, all wrong. Why didn't God do something? Why didn't God stop it from happening?" It's a cruel world, and even God's people are not above doing cruel things.

Still the story of cruelty and injustice persists. We see its evidence all around us and within us. A father walks out on his wife and children leaving them heart-broken, confused, and destitute. Children are abused and, in some places, simply abandoned by their parents. The physically and mentally disabled are slotted and dismissed by a society which does not know what to do with them. The poor are lumped together, and all are labeled as lazy. Sick and disabled veterans die while waiting for medical care from the healthcare system that is supposed to care for them. And globally you can see it in the despotism of dictatorial powers, sectional and religious hatred and violence, and the wholesale murder of the innocent and powerless.

If God shows any favor towards any one group over another in the scriptures, it is always to the powerless and the weak. God chose a group of slaves in Egypt to be the bearers of his blessing to the world. And when those chosen people forgot their calling and began the exploitation of the weak and powerless among themselves, God sent the prophets to show them the error of their ways and to summon them back to the paths of righteousness. When God sent his Son into the world, he was born to common people among the common people. Throughout his life and ministry Jesus was especially drawn to the marginalized, the ostracized, the sick, the suffering, and the most vulnerable. He was hardest on the self-satisfied, self-righteous people who ignored the suffering ones around them.

It would be easy to equate weakness and vulnerability with virtue and power and wealth with evil, and some people do. After all, in Luke's gospel Jesus says: "Blessed are you who are poor, for yours is the kingdom of God. Blessed are you who are hungry now, for you will be filled. Blessed are you who weep now, for you will laugh. Blessed are you when people hate you, and when they exclude you, revile you and defame you on account of the Son of Man. . . . But woe to you who are rich, for you have received your consolation. Woe to you who are full now, for you will be hungry. Woe to you who are laughing now, for you will mourn and weep." But weakness and vulnerability do not naturally equate to virtue and power and wealth with evil. That is neither true to reality nor true to God's judgment. No matter who you are, how much you have or how little you have, how faithful or unfaithful you are, you can find yourself, like Hagar, in a wilderness of want, fear and vulnerability not of your own choosing. Even you can be the victim of injustice. "Why me?" we sometimes wonder. "Why my child, my loved one?" "Why not?" may be the answer that comes back. It's a cruel and unpredictable world in which we live, and while we may bring some things on ourselves, others are simply thrust upon us. Bad things happen to the best of people. You know it and I do. Being a Christian does not guarantee any immunity to pain, or want, or hardship.

We may never understand some things, but of this assurance we can be certain: The Lord hears our cry and responds. When the water had run out and the bread was eaten, Hagar put her child in the shade of a bush and walked away and sat down by herself, for she could not bear to see him die. Can you imagine that kind of pain? Perhaps, you can. God heard the voice of the boy and through an angel spoke to Hagar: "Come, lift up your boy and hold him tight, for I will make a great nation of him." It was then that Hagar's eyes were opened, and she saw what her despair had kept her from seeing—a well of refreshing, life-renewing water. There are times in life when things seem so overwhelming that our eyes are blind to the springs of hope and life that may be around us, until, that is, the Lord, having heard our cry, opens our eyes to wells of unexpected life-sustaining water within our reach. It may be that peace that passes all understanding that comes to us when we at last put whatever it is that assails us into God's hands and trust in his care. It may be in the arrival into your life of someone who is able to do something and who actually cares about you and your problem. It may be in the gift of someone who says: "I don't have an answer for you, but I am here with you and will stay with you." Jesus assured his disciples and us: "Are not two sparrows sold for a penny? Yet not one of them will fall to the ground apart from your Father. And even the hairs of your head are all counted. So, do not be afraid; you are of more value than many sparrows."

It's a cruel story—this story of Hagar and Ishmael, but life can be cruel, unfair, and unjust at times, but in and through it all is the promise of God's presence, sustaining power, and gracious purpose being worked out in and through and for us.

Who Belongs Here?
Genesis 37:1-4, 12-28; Romans 10:5-15

Genesis 37:1-4, 12-28

Jacob settled in the land where his father had lived as an alien, the land of Canaan. This is the story of the family of Jacob. Joseph, being seventeen years old, was shepherding the flock with his brothers; he was a helper to the sons of Bilhah and Zilpah, his father's wives; and Joseph brought a bad report of them to their father. Now Israel loved Joseph more than any other of his children, because he was the son of his old age; and he had made him a long robe with sleeves. But when his brothers saw that their father loved him more than all his brothers, they hated him, and could not speak peaceably to him.

Romans 10:5-15

Moses writes concerning the righteousness that comes from the law, that 'the person who does these things will live by them.' But the righteousness that comes from faith says, 'Do not say in your heart, "Who will ascend into heaven?"' (that is, to bring Christ down) 'or "Who will descend into the abyss?"' (that is, to bring Christ up from the dead). But what does it say?

'The word is near you,
 on your lips and in your heart'

(that is, the word of faith that we proclaim); because if you confess with your lips that Jesus is Lord and believe in your heart that God raised him from the dead, you will be saved. For one believes with the heart and so is justified, and one confesses with the mouth

and so is saved. The scripture says, 'No one who believes in him will be put to shame.' For there is no distinction between Jew and Greek; the same Lord is Lord of all and is generous to all who call on him. For, 'Everyone who calls on the name of the Lord shall be saved.'

But how are they to call on one in whom they have not believed? And how are they to believe in one of whom they have never heard? And how are they to hear without someone to proclaim him? And how are they to proclaim him unless they are sent? As it is written, 'How beautiful are the feet of those who bring good news!'

To be truthful with you, I don't think that I would have liked Joseph at all. In our lesson for today he comes across as an arrogant, self-righteous, out-of-touch-with-the-real-world, pampered, tattletale pain in the neck. He was his father's favorite—there was no doubt about that—and his brothers resented him because of it. Indeed, they despised him and would have wasted no tears on him had he met his demise. In fact, they plotted to bring that about, and in our lesson for today they found the opportunity for which they had been waiting.

In our lives, too, there are people who, for one reason or another, we simply find unlikeable--or worse. Unlike Joseph's brothers, we may not wish them any harm, but at the same time we would not be sorry to see them just go away, or better yet get the comeuppance which is their due. Some years ago, when I was leaving one church to accept a call to another, friends from the Presbytery gave me a going-away dinner party. One member of the group, a lay leader in the Presbytery, confessed: "When I first met you, Dudley, I didn't like you at all. Only later when I got to know you did I discover that you are not such a bad fellow after all." He said it with a smile, but I couldn't have been more surprised. I wondered, though I didn't ask, what precisely had there been about me that he had found so unlikeable? Or was it something he projected on to me because of the way I looked, or talked, or the church I served? Even in the church there will be people we do not like and those who do not like us. We may see them as arrogant, rude, and entitled. We may find their life-styles, politics, or causes objectionable. They may have offended us or hurt us or someone we love.

While we would prefer to surround ourselves with people we like and who like us, that is not always possible. My mother used to remind me as a child, "You can pick your friends, but you can't pick your family." In other words, you belong to them, and they belong to you, and each has a responsibility to the other as family. The same is true of the church. We are not a loose confederation of relatively like-minded people. We may segregate ourselves into different denominations, different schools of theological thought and biblical interpretation; we may stand on opposite sides of what we understand to be critical issues, but we are still family. We belong to God in Jesus Christ and we belong to one another. At our best, we embrace each other as brothers and sisters in Christ in spite of our differences. At our worst, like Joseph's brothers, we plot the other's undoing. You can pick your friends, but not your family, and in this case, God has done the picking for us.

Robert Frost in his poem *The Death of the Hired Man* wrote of Silas, a ne'er-do-well laborer who in a time of need returned to the only place where he felt he might find a welcome. "Mary sat musing on the lamp-flame at the table, waiting for Warren. When she heard his step, she ran on tip-toe down the darkened passage to meet him in the doorway with the news and put him on his guard. 'Silas is back.' She pushed him outward with her through the door and shut it after her. 'Be kind,' she said. . . .. 'When was I ever anything but kind to him? But I'll not have the fellow back. I told him so last haying, didn't I? If he left then, I said, that ended it. What good is he? Who else will harbor him at his age for the little he can do?' . . . 'Warren,' she said, 'he has come home to die: You needn't be afraid he'll leave you this time.' 'Home,' he mocked gently. 'Yes, what else but home?' . . . 'Home is the place where, when you have to go there, they have to take you in. Go, look, see [him] for yourself, [she said] . . . . I'll sit and see if that small sailing cloud will hit or miss the moon.' Warren returned—too soon, it seemed to her, slipped to her side, caught up her hand and waited. 'Warren,' she questioned. 'Dead,' was all he answered."

While there are those who come home to the church when death is on the horizon, church is not simply a place to come to die, but rather it is the place to come to life, to be saved. In some theological circles, salvation is what rescues you from the yawning jaws of hell waiting to devour you at the end of your days. However, salvation might more appropriately be thought of as what rescues us today from the brokenness of this life and tomorrow rescues us from the nothingness of death. Martin Marty writes: "Salvation is 'being right with God,' becoming healthy and whole through the action of God. A new person comes to be where the old corrupt one had been. Salvation means being brought from the status of alien, the lost outsider, to adoption as a member of the family of God. Salvation means moving by God's initiative from being bound and blind to being free and seeing."[17] None of us is saved because of a good attitude, good works, or obedience to the rules. Like ne'er-do-well Silas, all that we have to call on is the goodness of the one who welcomes us home. Each of us comes empty-handed. Your place and mine in the Father's house come to us by faith in God's grace in Jesus Christ—by faith alone. We trust God to do for us what we cannot do for ourselves.

Eugene Peterson paraphrases a portion of our text from Romans in these words: "The word that saves is right here, as near as the tongue in your mouth, as close as the heart in your chest. It's the word of faith that welcomes God to go to work and set things right for us. . . . Say the welcoming word

---

[17] Martin Marty, *The Word: The People Participating in Preaching*, Fortress Press, 1984, p. 11

to God— 'Jesus is Master.'"[18] When we in faith give ourselves over to the lordship of Jesus Christ and trust him to do for us what we cannot do for ourselves, we are saved. "That's it," paraphrases Peterson. "You're not *doing* anything; you're simply calling out to God, trusting him to do it for you. That's salvation."

Such faith is not so much a destination as it is a journey. It is not so much a possession as a gift to be shared. Again and again Christ calls us out of ourselves into the world to share the good news that, "'Everyone who calls on the name of the Lord shall be saved.' But, how are they to call on one in whom they have not believed?" asks St. Paul. "And how are they to believe in one of whom they have never heard? And how are they to hear without someone to proclaim him? And how are they to proclaim him unless they are sent?" You and I are those who have been sent. That is the heart of our life and mission as the church, the people of God in Jesus Christ. It is as we focus on that mission and remain faithful to it that the church will grow, and in growing will draw in all sorts of people, some of them like us and some of them not. Some of them will be deserving, in our opinion, and some of them not; some we will like, and some we will not, but as the scripture reminds us: God shows no partiality, for "there is no distinction between Jew and Greek; the same Lord is Lord of all and is generous to all who call on him." There is no distinction between liberal or conservative, black or white, gay or straight, rich or poor,

---

[18] Eugene Peterson, *The Message*, NavPress, © Eugene Peterson, 2002

for we are all one in Christ. Each of us and all of us together are debtors to God's rich grace to us in him, and each of us have a place here.

Johnny Come Lately
Matthew 20:1-16

For the kingdom of heaven is like a landowner who went out early in the morning to hire laborers for his vineyard. After agreeing with the laborers for the usual daily wage, he sent them into his vineyard. When he went out about nine o'clock, he saw others standing idle in the market-place; and he said to them, "You also go into the vineyard, and I will pay you whatever is right." So they went. When he went out again about noon and about three o'clock, he did the same. And about five o'clock he went out and found others standing around; and he said to them, "Why are you standing here idle all day?" They said to him, "Because no one has hired us." He said to them, "You also go into the vineyard." When evening came, the owner of the vineyard said to his manager, "Call the labourers and give them their pay, beginning with the last and then going to the first." When those hired about five o'clock came, each of them received the usual daily wage. Now when the first came, they thought they would receive more; but each of them also received the usual daily wage. And when they received it, they grumbled against the landowner, saying, "These last worked only one hour, and you have made them equal to us who have borne the burden of the day and the scorching heat." But he replied to one of them, "Friend, I am doing you no wrong; did you not agree with me for the usual daily wage? Take what belongs to you and go; I choose to give to this last the same as I give to you. Am I not allowed to do what I choose with what belongs to me? Or are you envious because I am generous?" So the last will be first, and the first will be last.'

In his book *All Over but the Shoutin'* Rick Bragg tells the story of growing up dirt poor in the hills of north Alabama. If you read it, it will make you laugh out loud. It will also bring tears to your eyes. Most of the story centers on his mother, Margaret Marie Bragg. "Poor," he writes, "is all that she'd ever witnessed, tasted, been. She was not some steel magnolia thrust into alien poverty by a sorry man, but a woman who grew up with it. . . .. Her sisters wed men who worked hard, who bought land, homes, and cars that did not reek of spilt beer. Through their vows and some luck, they made good lives and had good things that had never been worn or used before. Momma, bless her heart, picked badly, and the years of doing without spun a single, unbroken thread through her childhood, her youth, her middle age, until the gray crept into her hair. . . The first memory I have [of her] is of a tall blond woman who drags a canvas sack along an undulating row of rust-colored ground, through a field that seems to reach into the back forty forever. I remember the sound it makes as it slides between the chest-high stalks that are so deeply, darkly green that they look almost black, and the smell of kicked-up dust and sweat. The tall woman is wearing a man's britches and a man's old straw hat, and now and then she looks back over her shoulder to smile at the three-year-old boy whose hair is almost as purely white as the bolls she picks, who rides the back of the six-foot-long sack like a magic carpet."[19] A hard way to scratch out a living, it is hand-to-mouth, day after day.

In this morning's Gospel lesson Jesus tells a story about another set of field hands. They, too, were poor, dirt poor. They, too, struggled day after day in the burning heat of the sun, like Margaret Marie Bragg, just to survive, to put a little food on the table. The first of them had gone into the field at the break of dawn. As the day passed, others joined them. These, too, were glad for the work, even if it wasn't a full day's work. Some of them came to the fields in the mid-morning, some mid-day, some mid-afternoon, and some even near to the close of day. When the light began to fade, the owner summoned his manager and had him pay the workers beginning with the last hired. Expecting to receive only that portion of the day's wages which they had actually earned, each was startled to receive a full day's wages. The hopes of those who had labored all day began to rise as each group of latecomers received a full day's wages. Surely, they were entitled to something more than a single day's pay! But then each of them received the same as the others—a day's wages, nothing more, nothing less. Disappointment stirred to indignation and indignation to anger. "These last worked only one hour and you have made them equal to us who have borne the burden of the day and the scorching heat," they objected. I think of Margaret Marie Bragg standing there with her little tow-headed boy in hand hopefully anticipating something that might go beyond

---

[19] Rick Bragg, *All Over but the Shoutin'*, (Paw Prints, 2008), 25, 23

providing bread for the table—maybe a pair of shoes or jeans with no holes in them. Then comes the disappointment, the crushing disappointment of receiving only what she was due, when those who worked so much less got so much more than *they* were due.

What happens in this parable is unfair. It's insulting. It's anything but equitable. Imagine what would happen if the world really functioned that way. I know there are those who think it should, but in reality, it would be disastrous. What would be the incentive for getting up and getting to work on time, putting in an honest day's labor, and giving your best, if you're going to be compensated the same for sleeping late, enjoying a leisurely breakfast, taking time to read the newspaper and do the crossword, run a few errands, and work out at the gym before showing up for work an hour before the close of business? Where is the merit, the fairness in that? Our whole economic system, indeed, our understanding of life, is based on a system of merit. You work hard in life, and you expect to enjoy the fruits of your labor. You live right and try to do what is right, and you expect to be treated right. Anything less is an injustice. This story, though, is not about world economic systems or the economy of human merit; it is about the extravagance of divine grace, which, in fact, impacts both.

While the law firm Harrell and Harrell might encourage you: "Don't settle for less than you deserve," grace is not about getting what you deserve. Grace is getting more than you deserve, more than you are due. Grace is being forgiven when you find it hard to forgive yourself. Grace is being loved and accepted when you don't love yourself anymore. Grace is a second chance and sometimes a third. Grace is the prodigal son being forgiven, welcomed home, and given a party. Grace is Jesus sitting down to dinner with tax collectors and sinners. Grace is forgiving a dying thief on the cross next to him and promising him a place in heaven. Grace does not erase justice, either divine or human, but tempers it.

Most of us have no problem with grace in general; it is grace in *particular* that bothers us, especially when it is extended to those who in our estimation don't deserve it. But who really does? Charles Cousar writes: "Divine grace is a great equalizer which rips away presumed privilege and puts all recipients on a par. That's hard to stomach when we have burdened ourselves with a merit system and want to see some reward for our labors. That's hard to stomach when we discover those guilty of wrongs we have long opposed (racism, sexism, colonialism, and the like) are brothers and sisters to whom the divine generosity has been shown. Grace no longer seems so sentimental."[20] It is radical, and sometimes it is offensive, but we, too, are debtors to grace. Who among us can honestly look at our lives and believe that we can merit God's love and a place in God's kingdom? Who among us can look at the cross of Christ and believe,

---

[20] Charles Cousar, *A Text for Preaching: Commentary Based on the NRSV Year A*, (Westminster/John Knox Press, 1995), 495

honestly believe, "I deserve this?" We are all debtors to grace. We all receive more than we deserve.

The debt, while not one we can repay or need to repay, is one that, in today's parlance we are called to "pay forward." As we have been loved by God in Christ, so are we called to love others. As we have been forgiven by God in Christ, so are we called to forgive others. As we have been blessed by the extravagance of God's grace in Christ, so, too, are we called to share an extravagant grace with others. That can be challenging; it can be difficult; it can be costly. It can cost us some of our pride; it can cost us the sweet taste of revenge; it can cost us the full measure of justice we believe we deserve; it can cost us the warmth of hanging on to the burning embers of unresolved anger; it can cost us a lot. Paradoxically, receiving grace can be equally as difficult, sometimes even more difficult, for it, too, can be costly. It entails confessing our wrongs, admitting our need, and our pride resists that.

The wonderful thing about God's grace in Christ is that it comes to us in such abundance that we not only have enough for ourselves but enough to share as well. Who in the circle of your life today could use some grace? Where in your own life do you need to accept some grace?

Practicing Love
John 15:9-17

As the Father has loved me, so I have loved you; abide in my love. If you keep my commandments, you will abide in my love, just as I have kept my Father's commandments and abide in his love. I have said these things to you so that my joy may be in you, and that your joy may be complete.

'This is my commandment, that you love one another as I have loved you. No one has greater love than this, to lay down one's life for one's friends. You are my friends if you do what I command you. I do not call you servants any longer, because the servant does not know what the master is doing; but I have called you friends, because I have made known to you everything that I have heard from my Father. You did not choose me, but I chose you. And I appointed you to go and bear fruit, fruit that will last, so that the Father will give you whatever you ask him in my name. I am giving you these commands so that you may love one another.

One of the joys for me in this ministry at Memorial is weekly chapel time with the children in our Presbyterian Day School. I share that pleasure with my three colleagues in ministry. I don't really know what their chapel programs are like, but I always share the Bible story of the day with the children first, then we sing a few songs like *Jesus Loves Me* and *He's Got the Whole World in His Hands*; and finally we conclude with a prayer in which I speak the words and they echo them. We talk a lot about love in chapel. If you were to ask a class of three-and four-year-old children to define love, they would probably just look at you, but they know what love is. Love is feeling wanted and secure. Love is getting tucked into bed at night with a kiss and a hug. Love is being comforted when you are hurt, encouraged when you are uncertain, made to feel protected when you are afraid. Love is having food to eat, a bed of your own, a roof over your head. It is being cared for and made to feel that you matter. These children know a lot about love because they have both been told "I love you" and shown that they are loved.

Jesus, too, talked a lot about love—God's love for us and our love for one another. In the waning hours of his life and one of the most intimate conversations he shared with his disciples, the admonition that he left with them had nothing to do with right doctrine or the organizational structure for mission and ministry, but was "this is my commandment, that you love one another, as I have loved you." While the Gospel calls us to love all people, here Jesus was speaking specifically to his disciples' love for one another. In the confusing days ahead, in the years, decades, and centuries that were to follow, the most important thing we can do, he told them, is to love one another as he has loved us. While Jesus had taught his disciples about the Father's love for him and his love for them, it was primarily in his example that they came to understand love. Love was taking children in his lap and blessing them when he could have been doing far more important things by the world's standards. It was pausing as he was being hurried along to the bedside of an important official's dying child to listen to and to heal a woman, a *nobody*, who needed him to listen as much as to heal her. It was sitting at table with tax collectors and "sinners." It was kneeling beside a woman about to be stoned to death for adultery, forgiving her, and challenging those who would kill her: "Let him who is without sin cast the first stone." It was healing the sick, casting out demons that distort human life, feeding the hungry, teaching, listening, and caring for hours on end. And ultimately it was bearing his cross to Calvary and dying in solitude and shame—dying even for those who condemned him to death. So would Jesus have us love one another in the community of faith—boldly, sacrificially, humbly, and without distinction.

That is hard sometimes, very hard, because, if we are honest about it, we don't always like each other very much, even within the church. We disagree with each other over both petty and significant matters. We say and do things that hurt each other and continue to eat away at us for years to come. Some of us here this morning bear wounds in our souls for things that happened to us or were said to us in church. And, beyond that there are some people whom we simply cannot bring ourselves to like, much less love, even in the church. Fortunately, love is not about what we feel but rather what we do. "In the Christian sense, love is not primarily an emotion but an act of the will," writes Frederick Buechner. "When Jesus tells us to love our neighbors, he is not telling us to love them in the sense of responding to them with a cozy emotional feeling. You can as well produce a cozy emotional feeling on demand as you can a yawn or a sneeze. On the contrary, he is telling us to love our neighbors in the sense of being willing to work for their well-being even if it means sacrificing our own well-being to that end, even if it means just leaving them alone. Thus, in Jesus' terms we can love our neighbors without necessarily liking them. In fact, liking them may stand in the way of loving them by making us overprotective sentimentalists instead of reasonably honest friends."[21]

One of the most important things that we can do to foster love for one another or to remove the obstacles that stand in the way of our love for one another is simply to listen to each other. "The first service that one owes to others in the [Christian] fellowship consists in listening to them," wrote Dietrich Bonhoeffer. "Just as love for God consists in listening to His Word, so the beginning of our love for our [brothers and sisters] is in listening to them. It is God's love for us that He not only gives us His Word but lends us His ear. So, it is His work that we do for our [brothers and sisters] when we learn to listen to them. Christians, especially ministers, so often think that they must always contribute something when they are in the company of others, that this is the one service they have to render. They forget that listening can be a greater service than

---

[21] Buechner, Frederick, *Wishful Thinking*, Harper and Row, 1973, p. 54

speaking."[22] I've had people come in to the church office and ask to speak to the pastor. Very often that means that they need or want some tangible service that the church may be able to provide, but every once in a while there is one who doesn't want any one particular *thing*, but rather someone simply to listen and pray. Such listening is especially important in those times when we disagree. Too often in such times we stop talking to each other and, if we do talk it, is not so much *with* one another as in opposition to one another. When the purpose is not to understand, but to win, our failure to listen to one another only widens the gap that divides. We will never all agree, but because Christ loves us we, too, strive to love one another.

The church's most profound and compelling witness to the love of God in Jesus Christ is not to be found in any prophetic declarations or in the glory and grandeur of our rites and buildings, but in who we are: a diverse community of people who love God in Jesus Christ and who love one another and who continually reach out to draw others into the circle of love and life which is ours in Jesus Christ. As the song reminds us, "They will know we are Christians by our love." Practice love; it will change your heart and maybe the heart of your neighbor as well.

---

[22] Dietrich Bonhoeffer *Life Together: The Classic Exploration of the Christian Community*, p. 97

Dry Bones
John 11:1-45

Now a certain man was ill, Lazarus of Bethany, the village of Mary and her sister Martha. Mary was the one who anointed the Lord with perfume and wiped his feet with her hair; her brother Lazarus was ill. So the sisters sent a message to Jesus, 'Lord, he whom you love is ill.' But when Jesus heard it, he said, 'This illness does not lead to death; rather it is for God's glory, so that the Son of God may be glorified through it.' Accordingly, though Jesus loved Martha and her sister and Lazarus, after having heard that Lazarus was ill, he stayed two days longer in the place where he was. . ... When Jesus arrived, he found that Lazarus had already been in the tomb for four days. Now Bethany was near Jerusalem, some two miles away, and many of the Jews had come to Martha and Mary to console them about their brother. When Martha heard that Jesus was coming, she went and met him, while Mary stayed at home. Martha said to Jesus, 'Lord, if you had been here, my brother would not have died. But even now I know that God will give you whatever you ask of him.' Jesus said to her, 'Your brother will rise again.' Martha said to him, 'I know that he will rise again in the resurrection on the last day.' Jesus said to her, 'I am the resurrection and the life. Those who believe in me, even though they die, will live, and everyone who lives and believes in me will never die. Do you believe this?' She said to him, 'Yes, Lord, I believe that you are the Messiah, the Son of God, the one coming into the world.'

. . . When Jesus saw her weeping, and the Jews who came with her also weeping, he was greatly disturbed in spirit and deeply moved.

He said, 'Where have you laid him?' They said to him, 'Lord, come and see.' Jesus began to weep. So the Jews said, 'See how he loved him!' But some of them said, 'Could not he who opened the eyes of the blind man have kept this man from dying?' Then Jesus, again greatly disturbed, came to the tomb. It was a cave, and a stone was lying against it. Jesus said, 'Take away the stone.' Martha, the sister of the dead man, said to him, 'Lord, already there is a stench because he has been dead for four days.' Jesus said to her, 'Did I not tell you that if you believed, you would see the glory of God?' So they took away the stone. And Jesus looked upwards and said, 'Father, I thank you for having heard me. I knew that you always hear me, but I have said this for the sake of the crowd standing here, so that they may believe that you sent me.' When he had said this, he cried with a loud voice, 'Lazarus, come out!' The dead man came out, his hands and feet bound with strips of cloth, and his face wrapped in a cloth. Jesus said to them, 'Unbind him, and let him go.'

Kneeling by the bedside, she held to her husband's lifeless hand with a vise-like grip, sobbing with unspeakable grief. He was all she had. They had no children, no other close family, and each other was all they had needed for years. Still a young pastor in my twenties, I knelt beside her and placed my arm around her and felt utterly useless. "Can these bones live?" I wondered. Not his—his body was already growing cold—but the bones of her broken life.

"Can these bones live?" God asked his spokesman Ezekiel, as the prophet, caught up in another of his visions, stood wide-eyed before a field strewn with bones, scores and scores of bones, picked clean by scavengers and bleached white by the sun. They were the bones of warriors who had rushed headlong into battle, savoring the taste of victory only to be swallowed in death and defeat. They were the bones of fathers and sons who gave their lives to protect their homes and families, villages and farms. Israel had been overwhelmed by the onslaught of the enemy. Jerusalem lay in ruins, the Temple reduced to a heap of rubble, and the brightest and best among the survivors had been taken into exile. Every symbol of Israel's national and religious identity had been obliterated. They had nothing; the future was bleak, at best, if not altogether hopeless.

I imagine Mary and her sister Martha felt much the same. Lazarus was not only their brother, but, in their culture, he was also their security, their support, and their future. When he was close to death, they had sent an urgent message to their friend Jesus to come as quickly as possible. If anyone could do anything to help, they knew he could, but Jesus lingered two more days where he was before making the trip to Bethany. In the meantime, Lazarus died. "Lord, if you had been here, my brother would not have died," Martha, and later Mary, chastised him. "Where were you? Why did you delay? Why did you ignore us and our need? He loved you."

Who among us has not, at one time or another, stood before the open grave of life as we have known it or as we had hoped it would become and wondered: "Can these bones live?" Can this marriage that began with such hopeful optimism and wonderful passion ever again pulse with life? . . . Will I ever live again, really live again in the wake of his death? Will the emptiness ever stop hurting? . . . My child is out of control and I have no idea what I can do. I've tried threatening, punishing, even pleading. What more is there? . . . What do you mean "downsizing"? I've given the best years of my life to this company. I can't be without a job. I have a family, a mortgage, bills to pay. How quickly, how unexpectedly our lives are changed, our hopes shattered, and our dreams dashed. Suddenly, through no fault of our own, we find ourselves cast into the uncertainty of life in a foreign land, and sometimes, like Israel, we may well lament: "Our bones are dried up, and our hope is lost; we are cut off completely." Can these bones live? Not a chance, or so it may seem in the moment.

That may well have been what Ezekiel himself thought about the situation he faced, but what he said in response to the Lord's query was: "Oh Lord God, you know"—a diplomatic answer, if ever there has been one. And God said to him: "Prophesy to these bones and say to them [to these people who think of themselves as being as good as dead]: O dry bones, hear the word of the Lord . . . I will cause breath to enter you, and you shall live. I will lay sinews on you, and will cause flesh to come upon you, and cover you again with skin . . . and you shall live." The future the Lord had planned for them was not at all the future of their fears. What Ezekiel was summoned to proclaim was the good news that, in spite of all the evidence to the contrary, God had not abandoned them. God was not back there in Jerusalem, or what had been Jerusalem, his spirit hovering over the pile of rubble that had been the Temple—his home—but God was with them in their exile, beside them in their perplexity, their bewilderment, their despair, and God was at work not only to sustain them but to bring about that which they believed was as likely as a heap of dry bones coming to life again. "Can these bones live?" Probably not, if it is entirely up to us. But in God's hands even a pile of sun-bleached bones can be the stuff of new life.

God has not abandoned us. There are times, I know, when we may well fear that he has, but still God enters into the lost places of this world, its dead and dying places, to bring life. Still God enters into the lost places of your life and mine, their dead and dying places, to bring healing and wholeness, new hope, new life. That may come in an act of complete deliverance—healing of an illness, renewal in your marriage, a new and better job, the lifting of a burden, or the shattering of the darkness of grief. It may come in the grace to carry a burden that isn't going to go away, the courage to face up to a problem that isn't going to change, or simply in the strength to persevere. God does not abandon us; God does not leave us to cope alone; God is at work to accomplish his good purpose in our lives. Even at the close of our lives—especially at the close of our lives—that is true. Jesus told Martha: "I am the resurrection and the life. Those who believe in me, even though they die, will live, and everyone who lives and believes in me will never die." Life's greatest opponent has been defeated. Of course, we still die, but from the perspective of the Christian Gospel, death is not merely or even ultimately a biological or physical phenomenon, but a spiritual one, and it is from this spiritual death that we have been delivered. "Death is man's separation from life," writes Alexander Schmemann, a scholar in the Orthodox tradition, "and this means from God who is the only Giver of life, who Himself is Life." Christ does not abolish or destroy physical death, "but he does infinitely more. By removing the sting of sin from death, by abolishing death as a spiritual reality, by filling it with Himself, with his love and life [God] makes death—what was the very reality of separation and corruption of life—into a shining and joyful 'passage' [or] passover—into fuller life, fuller communion, fuller love." [23]

"Can these bones live?" the Lord asked Ezekiel. "Do you see any hope for the future?" From the perspective of the never-ending conflict in the Middle East; the bickering of our national leaders in Washington; a denomination facing yet further declines in membership as a result of schism within the ranks; or, more personally, a house made empty by the death of a loved one; a parent's or spouse's descent into the

---

[23] Alexander Schmemann, *Of Water and the Spirit: A Liturgical Study of Baptism*, St. Vladimir's Seminary Press, 1997.

living death that is Alzheimer's disease; a child's struggle with addiction, or death's determined advance, the answer may well be: "No, not a chance." But from the perspective of Christian faith, the view is quite different, because our hope is not simply in ourselves or in the essential goodness of humanity; our hope is in a God who loved and loves us enough to give his Son to live among us, even to die for us so that we might live.

In God's eyes and God's hands, even the most impossible looking situations are filled with promise. Even a pile of dried up bones can be the stuff of life, and you and I, my brothers and sisters, are in God's hands.

Crossing Over Jordan
Joshua 3:7-17

The Lord said to Joshua, 'This day I will begin to exalt you in the sight of all Israel, so that they may know that I will be with you as I was with Moses. You are the one who shall command the priests who bear the ark of the covenant, "When you come to the edge of the waters of the Jordan, you shall stand still in the Jordan."' Joshua then said to the Israelites, 'Draw near and hear the words of the Lord your God.' Joshua said, 'By this you shall know that among you is the living God who without fail will drive out from before you the Canaanites, Hittites, Hivites, Perizzites, Girgashites, Amorites, and Jebusites: the ark of the covenant of the Lord of all the earth is going to pass before you into the Jordan. So now select twelve men from the tribes of Israel, one from each tribe. When the soles of the feet of the priests who bear the ark of the Lord, the Lord of all the earth, rest in the waters of the Jordan, the waters of the Jordan flowing from above shall be cut off; they shall stand in a single heap.'

When the people set out from their tents to cross over the Jordan, the priests bearing the ark of the covenant were in front of the people. Now the Jordan overflows all its banks throughout the time of harvest. So when those who bore the ark had come to the Jordan, and the feet of the priests bearing the ark were dipped in the edge of the water, the waters flowing from above stood still, rising up in a single heap far off at Adam, the city that is beside Zarethan, while those flowing towards the sea of the Arabah, the Dead Sea, were wholly cut off. Then the people crossed over opposite Jericho.

While all Israel were crossing over on dry ground, the priests who bore the ark of the covenant of the Lord stood on dry ground in the middle of the Jordan, until the entire nation finished crossing over the Jordan.

There are a number of things that I never thought I would live to see, and one of them is the inclusion of a hymn like "Shall We Gather at the River" in a Presbyterian hymnal. Presbyterian hymns are for the most part far more cerebral than this sentimental text that assures: "Soon we'll reach the shining river, soon our pilgrimage will cease; soon our happy hearts will quiver with the melody of peace." The text with its lovely, lilting melody calls us forward, inviting us to allow the river's "crystal tide" and "silver spray" to wash over us that we might at last "lay . . . every burden down." For those who struggle with pain in their final days, the hymn holds out the promise of physical and emotional relief. Soon it will be over. For those who have lost a loved one from their lives, it brings the comforting assurance that the one loved and lost lives yet in that "happy golden day." It's a comforting hymn.

Water, though, for all its soothing, refreshing, and renewing gifts, can also pose great difficulties. As it sustains life, it can also take life. As it has the power to move us along with its tides and currents to a desired location, it can also separate us from one another or from a dream long sought. At the end of their forty years of wilderness wandering and following the death of their leader Moses, the people of

Israel stood before the swollen spring waters of the Jordan River with only an untested and unproven Joshua as their leader. Just beyond the river lay the land of promise--a place where they could, at last, give up their semi-nomadic lifestyle, put down permanent roots, and enjoy the comforts of a home. They could see it, but between them and it rushed, deep and wide, the waters of the Jordan.

When my stepmother, who was always making plans for tomorrow even when those around her could plainly see that she wouldn't have many more tomorrows, finally lay dying, she asked to see me. Looking up at me from the bed which would be her deathbed, she said: "Dudley, I don't know how to do it." "How to do what?" I asked her. "How to die," she answered. "What do I do?" "I don't know," I admitted. "I've yet to be where you are, but I imagine that there really isn't anything that you can do or need to do. Just let go and let God take care of you, and when the time is right just take the hand of Jesus who promised: 'In my Father's house are many rooms . . . and because I go to prepare a place for you, I will come again to take you to myself, that where I am there you may be also.' (John 14:2-3) Just take his hand," I told her. I don't know if my words helped, but I hope they did.

Death is not something we think much about anymore. Except for hospice workers, I imagine pastors are among the few in our culture who spend much time on the banks of the Jordan with those preparing to pass over. Unlike physicians and other health professionals whose job is to stave off death at all costs—and those costs can be enormous both in financial and emotional terms—our job is to prepare the way so that when, as another poet put it, "Your last call comes serene and clear, calm may my answer be, Lord, I am here." For most of us, though, death has moved to the periphery of our lives and only occasionally intrudes. Unlike previous generations, we are rather distant from death as a part of the rhythm of human life. That is not altogether a bad thing, but it does leave us less than prepared to deal with it when it visits. There is a stanza from a hymn by St. Francis of Assisi, which we know as "All Creatures of Our God and King" that exults: "And you, most gentle sister death, waiting to hush our final breath: Alleluia! Alleluia! Since Christ our light has pierced your gloom, fair is the night that leads us home. Sing praises! Alleluia! Alleluia! Alleluia! Alleluia!" The phrase "gentle sister death" caught me by surprise when I first read these lines, for death is invited along with all of creation—sun and moon, water and fire—to share in a global song of praise to the Creator. Death is as much a part of living as birth. None of us lives forever in this mortal flesh. We were never so intended. What we fear about death, I think is the unknown: how do we die, and what lies beyond?

For some, death is merely the closing of the book of life. There is nothing more beyond what we can see and hear, touch and feel. In one moment, you are; in the next you are not. So much of the ritual surrounding death in contemporary culture reflects that as it focuses upon what was, rather than what now is and is to be. It is almost exclusively rear-view. Friends are invited to attend "celebrations of life" at the home of the deceased, at her favorite bar or favorite park. We find comfort in the gift of memory and in life shared together, and remembering, talking about the one who has died is an important part of grieving, but if that is all that there is, it is bittersweet. Yet there is something within us, at least in most of us, I think, that at a very fundamental level resists that notion. One of the classic prayers of the church declares: "We thank thee that deep within the human heart is an unquenchable trust that life does not end with the grave, but that the God who made us will care for us beyond the bounds of vision even as he has cared for us in this earthly world." The scripture reminds us that as Christians: "We do not grieve as those who have no hope" (1 Thess. 4:13) because we know there is One who has gone before us in this life and who through his own death and resurrection has won the victory over sin and death, transforming the end into an open door into the very presence of God.

We live not because there is some unquenchable flicker of life within us that lives on despite death, but because the God who made us and who loves us refuses to let us go. "Who shall separate us from the love of Christ?" (Romans 8:35) St. Paul rhetorically asks. And then he lists off some potential foes--tribulation, distress, persecution, famine, nakedness, peril or sword--and finally declares: "No! In all these things we are more than conquerors, for I am convinced that neither life nor death nor anything else in all creation will be able to separate us from the love of God in Christ Jesus our Lord." (Romans 8:37) Therein lies our hope in life and in death: we are the Lord's. While "sister death" will claim this mortal frame, nothing can wrest us from God's gracious and loving hold in Jesus Christ.

I can't tell you how to die. I'm still working on that one myself, but I can assure you, on good authority, that even though you and I die, and we relinquish those we love to death, it is not the end. As the twelve elders of Israel bore the ark of the covenant—God's earthly abode with the children of Israel—into the water to open the way to the Promised Land so Jesus Christ, God incarnate, has opened the way for us and for all who trust him. Grandmothers and grandfathers, mothers and fathers, husbands and wives, and children and friends whom we have loved and lost in death live on not merely in our memories but as members of that "great cloud of witnesses" who urge us on in the journey of faith and who await our arrival in the land of promise.

In Communion with the Saints
1 Thessalonians 4:13-18

But we do not want you to be uninformed, brothers and sisters, about those who have died, so that you may not grieve as others do who have no hope. For since we believe that Jesus died and rose again, even so, through Jesus, God will bring with him those who have died. For this we declare to you by the word of the Lord, that we who are alive, who are left until the coming of the Lord, will by no means precede those who have died. For the Lord himself, with a cry of command, with the archangel's call and with the sound of God's trumpet, will descend from heaven, and the dead in Christ will rise first. Then we who are alive, who are left, will be caught up in the clouds together with them to meet the Lord in the air; and so we will be with the Lord forever. Therefore encourage one another with these words.

What will become of those you love after you are gone? It's a question that bothers me sometimes, not that I have any doubts about the ability of those closest to me to carry on emotionally, spiritually, or physically, but, still, I wonder. None of us can control the future, and even the best laid plans of today can be undone tomorrow. That's what worries me sometimes. Worrying, of course, doesn't accomplish anything. You do the best you can do and entrust those you love to God's providential care. The Christians in Thessalonica, though, pondered a related, albeit different sort of question: what about those whom they had known and loved who had died? What had become of them?

The question arose out of the very eager expectation within the church that the Lord's advent was close at hand—so close that death was no longer a concern for them. Any moment now, they thought, Jesus would come again and take them to be with himself, but he had not yet come and friends and neighbors, brothers and sisters, parents, children, and spouses had died. What about them? What had become of them or would become of them? Would they remain forever dead in the grave, never to be known or seen again by those who loved them? Would those who were alive at the Lord's coming continue to live while these others who had known him and loved him, who had worshiped and served him alongside them, fade into the anonymity of a forgotten history? This question, this unknown, only served to intensify the grief they felt. "We do not want you to be uninformed, about those who have died," the apostle reassures them, "so that you may not grieve as others who have no hope." He then proceeds to sketch a picture intended to bring them comfort and solace, but which in our time seems only embarrassingly naïve: "The Lord himself, with a cry of command, with the archangel's call and with the sound of God's trumpet, will descend from heaven, and the dead in Christ will rise first. Then we who are alive, who are left, will be caught up in the clouds together with them to meet the Lord in the air."

Passages like this, I suppose, are what give impetus to bumper stickers like: "In case of rapture, this car will be unmanned," and on-line services such as "Eternal Earth-Bound Pets, USA." "You've committed your life to Jesus. You know you're saved. But when the Rapture comes what's to become of your loving pets who are left behind? Eternal Earth-Bound Pets takes that burden off your mind. . .. For $135.00 we will guarantee that should the Rapture occur within ten (10) years of receipt of payment, one pet per residence will be saved. Each additional pet at your residence will be saved for an additional $20.00 fee. A small price to pay for your peace of mind and the health and safety of your four-legged and feathered friends." By contrast, "You've Been Left Behind" gives you one last opportunity to reach your lost family and friends For Christ. Imagine being in the presence of the Lord and hearing all of heaven rejoice over the salvation of your loved ones. . .. Get one last message to the lost, at a time when they might just be willing to hear it for the first and last time." You've Been Left Behind assures its clients: "We have set up a system to send documents by the email, to the addresses you provide, 6 days after the 'Rapture' of the Church. This occurs when 3 of our 5 team members scattered around the U.S fail to log in over a 3-day period. Another 3 days are given to fail safe any false triggering of the system." The cost is only $14.95 per year. As P.T. Barnum ostensibly said, "There's a sucker born every minute."

It would be easy simply to disregard such passages as this in Scripture or to surrender them to the likes of Eternal

Earth-Bound Pets and You've Been Left Behind, but these passages have a word we need to hear, and our world needs to hear. This is apocalyptic language, and as such it has more in common with the language of poetry than that of scientific analysis. It does not so much seek to detail a specific event yet to occur—"this is how it will unfold"—as it does to affirm that which goes beyond the power of words fully to describe. It hints at larger truths. The issue here is power and who has it. Is death indeed the last of us? Was Job correct, though perhaps a bit too pessimistic, when he lamented: "A mortal born of woman, few of days and full of trouble, comes up like a flower and withers, flees like a shadow and doesn't last . . . There is hope for a tree, if it is cut down, that it will sprout again and that its shoots will not cease . . . but mortals die and are laid low." (Job 14:1, 2, 7, 10) Is the best for which we can hope a cure or therapy that will extend our lives yet a little longer, even if all we are extending is the suffering? We simply aren't made to last forever. Even with the best care, the most expensive care, ultimately each of us will succumb to death's power.

Though death will most certainly claim us, what this and other passages assure us is that death does not have the final word over us, and that assurance is anchored not in some spark of vitality within human life that is immune to death's power, but in the victory of Jesus Christ over sin and death. "Jesus' resurrection," writes New Testament scholar Beverly Gaventa, "is not an isolated event, a single rabbit God pulls out of the hat to demonstrate that Jesus is in fact the Christ. The resurrection is directly connected with God's final triumph and with the lives of all human beings."[24] Because Christ lives, we too shall live. Not even the power of death may separate us from the love of God made manifest in his life, death, and resurrection. "Who shall separate us from the love of Christ?" asks St. Paul. "Shall tribulation or distress or persecution or famine or nakedness or peril or sword? No! In all these things we are more than conquerors through him who loved us. . . .. For I am sure that neither death nor life . . . nor anything else in all creation will be able to separate us from the love of God in Christ Jesus our Lord." (Romans 8:35, 37)

"All the major Christian creeds affirm belief in resurrection of the body," writes Frederick Buechner. "In other words they affirm the belief that what God in spite of everything prizes enough to bring back to life is not just some disembodied echo of a human being but a new and revised version of all the things which made him the particular human being he was and which he needs something like a body to express: his personality, the way he looked, the sound of his voice, his peculiar capacity for creating and loving, in some sense his face."[25] Christians die like anyone else. The difference is that because of God's life-giving love in Jesus Christ, we may face death not merely with resignation, or, worse yet, a sense of despair and defeat, but

---

[24] Beverly Roberts Gaventa, *Interpretation: First and Second Thessalonians*, (John Knox Press, 1998), p. 64
[25] Frederick Buechner, *Wishful Thinking: A Theological ABC*, (Harper and Row, 1973), pp. 42, 43)

with hope, a hope anchored in the victory of Christ over all that would ever separate us from God.

Still we grieve, though, and well we should. It is what enables us to cope with inestimable loss, as it frees us to give expression to pain and sorrow that reach to the very depths of the human soul. What distinguishes us is not immunity to loss and grief but hope in the midst of it. Those whom we have loved and lost, we will see again, and when we ourselves confront our own mortality, it will be with the assurance that what awaits us is not merely an empty grave and the dark of nothingness, but a new beginning, a shining and joyful passage into fuller life, fuller joy, fuller love in company with all the saints.

On this Sunday after All Saints' Day we remember with gratitude the saints who have walked beside us, who have shared our lives, and those who have walked before us and whose faith, love and stewardship of life prepared the way for us. We remember them with gratitude, but we also celebrate a communion in Christ with them that not even death can sever, for not only will we *be* together with the Lord, but we *are* together with the Lord. Samuel Wesley wrote of the church: "Yet she on earth hath union with God the Three in One, and mystic sweet communion with those whose rest is won; O happy ones and holy! Lord, give us grace that we, like them, the meek and lowly, on high may dwell with Thee."

www.ingramcontent.com/pod-product-compliance
Lightning Source LLC
Chambersburg PA
CBHW052132110526
44591CB00012B/1690